W9-DFF-617

twins

Dr. Carol Cooper & Katy Hymas

twins

Canadian Edition

the **practical** and **reassuring guide** to **pregnancy**, **birth**, and the **first year**

Project Editor Laura Palosuo
Editor Claire Tennant-Scull
Canadian Editor Barbara Campbell
Designer Saskia Janssen
Photographer Ruth Jenkinson
Photography Art Direction Peggy Sadler
Production Editor Andy Hilliard
Senior Production Controller Seyhan Esen
Creative Technical Support Sonia Charbonnier
Managing Editor Penny Smith
Managing Art Editor Marianne Markham
Category Publisher Peggy Vance

DK INDIA
Senior Editor Alicia Ingty
Editor Mahima Barrow
Art Editor Ira Sharma
Assistant Art Editors Tanya Mehrotra, Pooja Verma
DTP Designers Sourabh Challariya, Anurag Trivedi
Managing Editor Glenda Fernandes
Managing Art Editor Navidita Thapa

First Canadian Edition, 2012
Dorling Kindersley is represented in Canada by
Tourmaline Editions Inc.
662 King Street West, Suite 304
Toronto, Ontario M5V 1M7

12 13 14 10 9 8 7 6 5 4 3 2 1
001—183080—May/2012

Published in Great Britain by Dorling Kindersley Limited

Library and Archives Canada Cataloguing in Publication
Cooper, Carol, 1951-
    Twins / Carol Cooper, Katy Hymas. -- 1st Canadian ed.
Includes index.
ISBN 978-1-55363-182-8
    1. Multiple pregnancy. 2. Twins. 3. Multiple birth.
4. Infants--Care. I. Hymas, Katy II. Title.
RG567.C66 2012   618.2'5   C2011-906861-3

DK books are available at special discounts when purchased
in bulk for corporate sales, sales promotions, premiums, fund-raising, or
educational use. For details, please contact specialmarkets@tourmaline.ca.

Color reproduction by MDP, United Kingdom
Printed and bound in China by Leo Papers Ltd

Discover more at
www.dk.com

Contents

INTRODUCTION 6

YOUR PREGNANCY
Finding out 10
Twins demystified 12
Nutrition 14
Exercise 16
Your changing body 20
Your developing babies 24
Prenatal appointments and tests 28
Common symptoms 32
Possible complications 36

PREPARING FOR YOUR BABIES' ARRIVAL
Your hospital bag 40
What to buy 42
Childbirth classes 46
Emotional preparation 48
Pregnancy and work 50

LABOR AND BIRTH

Birth: the lowdown 54
Your birth plan 58
Premature babies 60
The hospital environment 62
Presentation of twins 64
Pain relief 66
Vaginal delivery 68
Cesarean birth 70

YOUR BABIES' ARRIVAL

Your new babies 76
Bonding 78
Feeding twins 80
Practical help 86
Special Care and Neonatal
    Intensive Care 88
How you might be feeling 90

THE YEAR AHEAD

Your babies' development 94
Relationships with your babies
    and partner 98
Dressing babies 102
Bathing, cleaning, and changing 104
Sleep 106
Crying 110
At home 112
Outings and vacations 114
Starting twins on solids 116
Keeping your babies healthy 120
The first birthday 122

RESOURCES 124

INDEX 125

ACKNOWLEDGMENTS 128

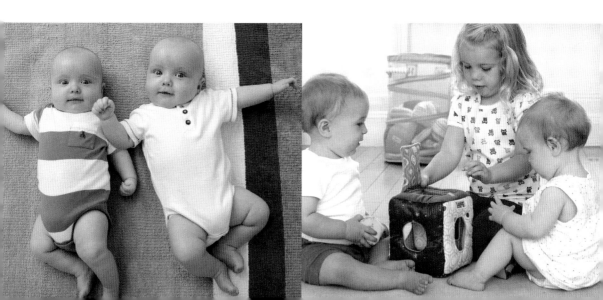

Hello from Carol

Having a baby is always special, doubly so if you're expecting twins. The thrill of anticipating two bundles of joy and the rewards of raising two special little people more than outweigh the challenges along the way. But at the start of your extraordinary adventure there are bound to be questions and concerns.

The human body is designed for having just one baby at a time, so you'll need to adjust for this. Whether or not this is your first pregnancy, you'll also have questions about managing day-to-day when your twins arrive.

Rest assured there are solutions that will suit your circumstances, ones that aren't always obvious at the time. I already had a toddler when my twins were born, and found the learning curve very different the second time around.

Here's where this book comes in. While my co-author Katy contributes her enthusiasm and know how, I offer a fusion of my professional skills and my personal experience of raising my amazing family.

I hope this book provides the information and encouragement you need to make the most of this exhilarating time.

Carol Cooper

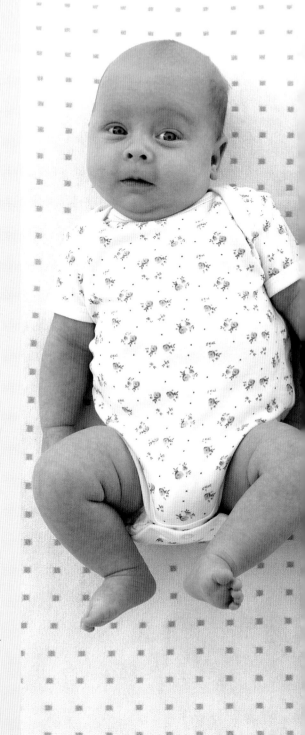

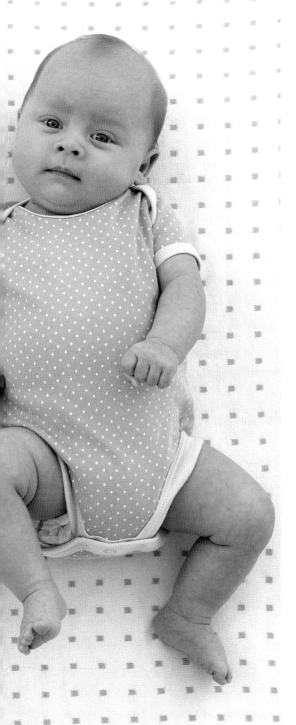

Hello from Katy

However and whenever you discovered you were carrying twins I am sure it was a shock, but you now have two teeny-tiny tickets to the best club in town—the Multiple Moms club. Congratulations!

As twin moms ourselves, Carol and I knew what sort of book we wanted to write—one we would have found most useful during our early twin days (or should that be our early twin daze?!). We hope that this book is a reassuring hug, a job-well-done handshake, and a reliable reference for you throughout your pregnancy and the first year.

Becoming a parent is life changing, be it to one baby or two, and there is no one-size-fits-all guide to how to do it. The information, advice, and tips within this book will give you knowledge, answers, pointers, and ideas to help you and your new family get off to a confident start.

There will be moments of panic and moments of pride throughout your twin adventure, but remember that you will get to know your babies better than anyone else. By the end of year one, you will have become your own expert, able to advise others on their twin journey.

Good luck, have fun, and enjoy your two new bundles of love!

Katy Hymas

Your pregnancy

Finding out

Home pregnancy tests do not show two blue lines if you are expecting twins so your "Twin Mom" status was probably confirmed at your doctor's office. Congratulations, you are not having a baby, you are having a family!

A new you, plus two!

If this is your first pregnancy, the whole experience will be new. If you have already experienced a singleton pregnancy, you may be aware of some differences, but as each pregnancy is unique, not all of these differences are necessarily the result of carrying two babies.

Being large for your gestational age is often a clue that you may be carrying more than one baby, but if this is your first pregnancy you will not have had a "normal" belly bump for comparison. If it is your second pregnancy, perhaps you expected to look and feel larger this time around.

You may have had your suspicions that you were carrying two babies if you underwent IVF, if there is a history of twins in your family, and/or if you experienced exaggerated pregnancy symptoms due to the double dose of hormones in your body. Multiple moms do not always have a more difficult pregnancy than their singleton counterparts, so don't assume the worst!

Discovering the duo

Twin moms often vividly remember the moment they discovered they were carrying two babies—a story that will no doubt be recounted many a time as the babies grow up. Perhaps your ultrasound tech looked serious and studied the screen intently before telling you what the scan had revealed? Or perhaps your ultrasound tech smiled right away and you knew that your suspicions were about to be confirmed? The emotional roller coaster of coming to terms with the twin news no doubt started the minute you were told!

Test results Finding out you're pregnant can be one of the most joyous times in your life, and a guarantee of coming changes in your lifestyle.

Telling others

Because of the increased likelihood of amplified side effects, you may discover you are having twins early on in your pregnancy. You may find out early due to IVF-related monitoring or a scan to check the cause of accelerated growth or exaggerated symptoms. Many women wait three months before sharing news of their pregnancy because the chances of miscarriage are higher during the first trimester. It can also be fun to keep your pregnancy secret initially and can be the start of a parental bonding process with your partner.

It may take longer for you to come to terms with the idea of a twin pregnancy and you might want to have some time to gather your thoughts without having to deal with other people's opinions about the news. You might feel shocked and overwhelmed to learn you are carrying two babies, and well-meaning but insensitive comments such as "How on earth will you manage?" are not helpful.

Telling older children that they will soon have not one but two new siblings can seem daunting, and their age(s) will affect when and how you share the news. It is worth waiting until the second trimester, when the pregnancy is well established, to share the news with older siblings. Ensure you are positive and clear when you tell them. Children are perceptive and likely to be aware of the changes in your mood before you talk to them about what is going on; by telling them about the twins early, you include them and ensure they feel a part of the new family dynamic.

Any pregnancy is special and the fact that you are nurturing two babies is to be celebrated. Speak to other twin moms who understand the emotional and physical journey you are about to embark on—you are at the start of a life-long adventure!

Having discovered that you are carrying two babies you may develop a "twin radar" and find that you see twins everywhere. Don't be afraid to approach other moms of multiples—they will vividly remember the mixture of apprehension and excitement that you may be feeling and can offer advice and tips. Be reassured to see twin families out and about and having fun, just as you will be in a few short months.

Twin discovery Knowing you're having twins can be exciting and daunting. Give yourself some time to come to terms with the news before sharing it with others.

Twins demystified

Twins are always fascinating, and doubly so when you know you're going to have them! There are lots of different myths and beliefs about twins, but just a few facts that you should know.

Same but different Your twins might look identical but they may not be exactly the same size and weight.

Why am I having twins?

Many factors make you more predisposed to conceive twins. A close family history of twins, especially on your mother's side, means that you are more likely to have twins yourself. Women over 35 also tend to have more fraternal twins than younger women, because they are more likely to produce two eggs at once instead of just one. Then there are fertility treatments such as ovulation induction and IVF (if more than one embryo is transferred).

Geography plays a part, too. While twins are fairly common in Nigeria, they're relatively rare in Japan and the rest of Southeast Asia. This may be linked with natural hormones in the diet, but some regional differences are harder to explain: Northern Ireland, for instance, has seen an inexplicably large rise in multiple births over the last few years.

Taller and better-nourished women tend to bear more twins, but there are also other less tangible influences, such as general fertility. If you became pregnant very easily, you are more prone to conceive two at once. But the bottom line is that nobody can predict exactly who will get twins. As with so much else to do with having children, there is a large element of chance. You could just say you're having twins because you're special!

What type of twins will I have?

Overall, about one in every 90 pregnancies is a twin pregnancy. And there are two distinct types of twins. Identical twins come from one fertilized egg (zygote) that splits very early on in pregnancy. Technically, the term is monozygotic (MZ) twins but it's usual just to call them identical. MZ twins have the same DNA and can be as alike as the proverbial peas in a pod. But as with peas, if you look very closely, you're bound to spot a few small differences.

Fraternal twins come from two separate eggs (ova) that were released at the same ovulation time and then fertilized by two different sperm. They're no more alike than any other two siblings but of course they're the same age. Here, the technical term is dizygotic (DZ) twins, though it is common to call them fraternal twins. Unlike MZ twins, they can be of different sexes—in fact, about half of all fraternal twins are boy-girl pairs.

If you've got a mixed-sex pair, then your twins are obviously not identical. But in many cases you may not know until they're born whether they're identical or not. Even then, it can be hard to tell unless you have DNA testing (so called zygosity testing).

One placenta or two?

Many people think that if you have just one placenta, it must mean your twins are identical. But this isn't necessarily so. Two placentas can merge very close together and fuse into one. Also, a fertilized egg that splits early on can produce two placentas, so the number of placentas isn't linked with the number of eggs. Even some doctors don't always realize this, so you're one up on them already.

What will my twins be like?

Whichever type of twins you have, it is good to remember that each baby will be an individual, with a distinct personality and unique physical characteristics. Having the same DNA doesn't make two people exactly the same—even identical twins don't have the same fingerprints or iris patterns. While they have the same color hair, the way it grows can be different, and so too can the shape of the head. This is because environment

has an impact and your babies' environment is present long before you meet them. In the uterus, conditions aren't exactly the same for each twin. One will be closer to the sound of your beating heart or your gurgling stomach, while the other may be closer to your dominant hand. Twins can get subtly different amounts of nourishment from the placenta, too. The bottom line is that, whether your twins came from one egg or two, they will be separate little people.

Twin statistics

Twin births

- In Canada, more than 4,000 sets of twins are born every year, and about 95 percent of all multiple births are twins
- About one-third of twins are MZ (identical)
- Two-thirds of twins are DZ (fraternal)

Average pregnancy length

- Singletons: 40 weeks
- Twins: 37 weeks

Average birth weight

- Singletons: 7 lb 7 oz (3.5 kg)
- Twins: 5 lb 5 oz (2.5 kg)

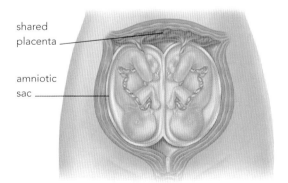

One egg Identical twins come from the same egg and may share a placenta, but they usually have a sac each.

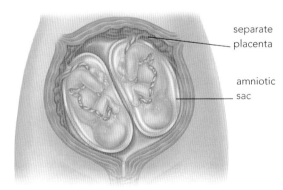

Two eggs Fraternal twins come from two eggs. There's often a placenta for each baby.

Nutrition

Not only will a healthy diet help you stay fit and well during pregnancy, it will give your babies the best start in life, too.

Staying hydrated

Keeping properly hydrated prevents headaches, constipation, urinary tract infections, and contractions, so it is worth the effort. The color of your urine will let you know how you are doing: it should be a pale straw color; any darker and it is a sign that you need to drink more. Add lemon or a slice of fruit or cucumber to water to keep it interesting and help you reach your quota. Juices and other liquids count, but limit your intake of caffeine to three or four cups a day.

Your dietary needs

Your body needs an additional 600 calories per day during a twin pregnancy—only 300 more than you would consume for a singleton pregnancy. This amount should help you to achieve the target weight gain during your pregnancy. If you have any concerns about pregnancy weight gain (either too much or too little), speak to your doctor.

A healthy pregnancy diet includes a variety of foods, and can include cake—just not a lot of it! The additional calories should come from a range of essential food groups and nutrients, including healthy fats, carbohydrates, protein, calcium, and iron. Make sure that the bulk of your diet is made up of fresh fruit and vegetables, whole grains, and calcium.

Vegetarian and special diets

If your diet is varied and balanced, it is possible to consume enough nutrients for your growing babies with a vegetarian diet, but it may be worthwhile to speak to your doctor to make sure your meals are not lacking anything. Vegan and restricted diets

Vegetables and fruit Packed with vitamins and minerals, the fiber also helps to keep constipation at bay.

Carbohydrates Whole grains, such as whole-wheat bread, are also a good source of fiber.

Protein Fish and meat are good sources of protein, essential for your growing babies.

resulting from food intolerances may benefit from supplements to ensure you are not missing essential nutrients. Again, your doctor will be able to advise you.

Supplements

Folic acid can help prevent birth defects. Foods, such as some breakfast cereals, are fortified with folic acid, but a supplement of 400 mcg starting from when you stop using birth control and taken throughout your pregnancy will ensure you consume the right amount.

Vitamin D is important for bone health. Sunlight and oily fish are good sources, but as not many foods contain it, consider a pregnancy supplement with the required amount of 15 mcg a day.

The recipe rule book

- Cook meat and poultry thoroughly. Make sure surfaces and utensils (and your hands!) used to prepare raw meat are washed well. Use a separate cutting board for raw meats.
- Don't eat liver or liver products since these are high in vitamin A and may harm your babies.
- Wash salad, fruit, and vegetables to remove all traces of soil/chemicals used during farming.
- Cook eggs thoroughly. The white and yolk should be solid to prevent salmonella food poisoning. Avoid foods containing raw or undercooked eggs.
- Avoid pâté and mold-ripened soft cheeses such as Brie, Camembert, and goat cheese because of the risk of listeria infection.
- Hard cheese is fine, and soft cheeses such as mozzarella, cottage cheese, and cheese spreads are fine as they are made from pasteurized milk.
- Drink pasteurized or UHT milk. Unpasteurized goats' or sheep's milk and products made from them are to be avoided.
- Nuts are a great source of energy and protein, and there is no evidence to suggest that eating peanuts when pregnant increases the likelihood of your babies developing allergies later in life. However, if you have a family history of nut allergies, speak to your doctor.
- Cooked fish is a great pregnancy food but some species need to be avoided as they may contain high levels of pollutants that can damage your babies' nervous systems. It is best to avoid swordfish and marlin, and limit the amount of tuna you eat.

Doctor's advice

Alcohol and tobacco

The advice from Health Canada and other health agencies on alcohol consumption is that there is no known amount of alcohol that is safe to drink while pregnant. Research shows that even modest drinking raises the risk of miscarriage. Heavy drinking can damage a baby permanently and even cause learning and other difficulties—so-called fetal alcohol syndrome. But if you did have the occasional drink before you knew you were expecting, you're unlikely to have put your babies at risk.

Cigarettes, in addition, are bad for babies in any quantity. Each puff you take makes your babies' heart race, robs them of oxygen, and raises the risk of miscarriage. Smoking is also linked with premature labor, stillbirth, and the risk of having a small, sickly baby. Babies born to women who smoke are more likely to have birth complications, sudden infant death syndrome (SIDS—also known as crib death), and asthma. Since you're carrying twins, it's doubly important not to smoke in while you are pregnant and to stay away from others that do. If you need help to quit, talk to your doctor.

Exercise

During your twin pregnancy you are allowed to eat more and rest more than you normally would, but don't forget that it's still important to get some exercise!

Ready, set, go!

Whether you were a regular gym rat or a couch potato pre-pregnancy, the new you has two very good reasons to focus on fitness. The safest way to ensure you are working out at a pregnancy-friendly level is to see whether you are still able to hold a conversation while you exercise.

Exercise will help you feel better and give you more energy. Staying fit and healthy can help you maintain your energy levels during and after birth.

Strong support

As your pregnancy progresses and your weight changes, your center of gravity will shift, making you more susceptible to losing your balance, particularly once you enter the second trimester. Retaining good posture is one way to counteract this. Your babies will be very well protected by the amniotic sac if you do fall, but prevention is the best form of protection!

What to avoid

Once you enter the fourth month of your pregnancy, your uterus will have grown significantly and the weight of it, when you lay on your back, can press against the vena cava and reduce blood flow to the heart. This leaves you feeling dizzy and light-headed, and your babies with a reduced oxygen supply. For this reason, avoid lying on your back during exercise or rest. Lie on your side for comfort and safety.

Your ligaments will soften during pregnancy due to a hormone called relaxin. This allows your bones to spread for the birth of your babies. It does, however, make your joints more vulnerable, so avoid jerky or bouncy exercises while pregnant. For the same reason, be careful when stretching.

Swimming A pregnancy-friendly exercise, but don't overly exert yourself. Ensure you stay hydrated by drinking lots of water before and after your swim.

Standing stretches

Stretching can be done in the comfort of your own home and helps to reduce some pregnancy-related complaints. It will enhance your flexibility and help you relax. Consider doing these simple exercises at the same time each day—you just need a little space and some comfortable clothing.

Stretch up Raise your arms above your head, keeping your elbows straight and the palms of your hands facing each other.

Stretch out Lower your arms out to your sides, keeping your upper back straight and your shoulders down. Look straight ahead.

Stretch behind Bring the backs of your hands together as far as possible behind your back. Hold for at least 20 seconds.

Pelvic floor

The additional weight you are carrying with a twin pregnancy places extra pressure on your pelvic floor. By strengthening it, you can reduce the likelihood of urine leakage. To know which muscles you need to strengthen, imagine the muscles you would use to stop urine mid-flow, then practice squeezing them throughout the day. If you can do it without raising your eyebrows, no one will ever know!

Walking

Walking can help increase cardiovascular health and reduce swollen ankles. Be sensible; don't wear high heels and head for the hills! Wear flat shoes and opt for easy terrain. Remember to take your water bottle.

Swimming

It is worth waddling to the swimming pool because you will be rewarded with a feeling of weightlessness when in the water. It will also protect your joints and ligaments and prevent you from overheating. Swimming can also help reduce swelling and ease the discomfort of varicose veins. Be careful getting in and out of the pool, and ensure you drink plenty of water before and after working out so that you don't become dehydrated.

Your pregnancy

Yoga and Pilates

Both yoga and Pilates help with flexibility and muscle tone. It is important that your teacher is aware you are carrying twins because certain positions, such as lying flat on your back or on your belly, are not appropriate.

Ready, set, stop

If you experience uterine contractions, vaginal bleeding, or fluid leakage during or after exercise contact your doctor to check that everything is OK.

Make sure you stay hydrated by drinking before, during, and after your workout, and make sure you do not get too hot. A high core temperature can adversely affect your babies.

Adrenaline junkies, hit the pause button! Avoid contact sports and activities where there is a high risk of falling, such as horseback riding or skiing. Do not do sit-ups, deep squats, or hold your breath during any activity, and do not participate in any activities that expose you to the risk of even mild abdominal trauma.

After birth it is generally safe for you to resume exercise at around four to six weeks after a normal birth and eight weeks after a cesarean delivery, but listen to what your body tells you and take advice

Sitting stretches

Shoulder stretches and ankle rotations can be done anywhere, but you might want to save the lying down stretch until you get home! If you feel better stretching regularly, then this healthy habit may stay with you after the birth.

Shoulder circles Stand or sit and rotate your shoulders backward and downward in an exaggerated circle. This will encourage you to sit tall.

Ankle rotations While sitting, lift one leg and rotate your ankle in both directions, then switch legs. This exercise will help reduce puffy feet.

Relax Lie on the floor with your legs raised against the wall. Shuffle your bottom as close to the wall as possible and take slow, deep breaths.

from your doctor if you are unsure whether you are ready to dust off your sneakers.

Know your limits

While it is safe to exercise during a twin pregnancy, you will increase in size more rapidly than women expecting one baby, and this may mean that some forms of exercise will become uncomfortable earlier in your pregnancy. Whatever exercise you do, stop if you feel at all unwell. The following symptoms are signs that you should stop and rest:

- dizziness
- headaches
- shortness of breath
- palpitations
- nausea
- blurred vision
- feeling unwell

Consult your doctor if these symptoms persist or if you have vaginal bleeding. Because twin pregnancies are more likely to end prematurely it is advisable not to do any vigorous exercise after 28 weeks. The third trimester can be especially tiring, so it is unlikely you will want to anyway.

Do not be tempted to exercise to lose weight or suddenly become a fitness fanatic. During pregnancy your objective is to help your body to help itself—gentle moderate exercise will leave you feeling fantastic (thank you endorphins!) without the risk of injury to you or your babies.

After pregnancy you may have mixed feelings about your post-baby-bump body but try not to put too much pressure on yourself to regain your figure right away. Breast-feeding and the general activity levels involved with taking care of two babies will help you to lose any pregnancy weight. After the first few weeks you may feel ready to do a little more, but try to set realistic goals. Begin with some low-impact exercise, such as walking, and slowly increase the amount you do each time.

Doctor's advice

Hidden benefits

Exercising in pregnancy does a lot more than just pass the time and keep you fit. It can help you socialize and make new friends, especially if you take up activities with other moms-to-be. It can also reduce the minor symptoms of pregnancy, like constipation and insomnia. It's even suggested that exercise reduces the risk of high blood pressure and pregnancy-related diabetes.

Perhaps the best news of all is that keeping physically active may help you and your babies during labor. There's evidence that women who exercise regularly have shorter labors and fewer complications. Of course, you can't count on that happening, especially since you're having twins. But it's good to know that something as simple as exercise could help you give your babies a great start.

You don't need to clad your twin belly in lycra or do a formal class—maintaining an active lifestyle during pregnancy can be factored into your everyday chores and could simply include walking to and from the bus stop. You might want to consider getting off a stop earlier if you are feeling energetic. Stick to a comfortable pace and remember to wear appropriate footwear.

Your "nesting instinct" may inadvertently help you stay fit and healthy; moving boxes of baby items and making sure cupboards are organized and floors clean are all activities likely to raise your heartbeat. Make sure you do not overly exert yourself since housework can be deceptively intensive and you must be wary of lifting, bending, and pushing as you move through your pregnancy.

Your changing body

Expect everyone to have an opinion on the size of your belly. It is likely to be deemed either too big or too small, but rest assured the two little people who call it home will think it is just right.

From here to maternity

You may not always feel at your most attractive during your pregnancy, but it is worth documenting belly growth for posterity with an assortment of photos, videos, and plaster molds. Believe it or not, you are likely to become nostalgic later on for your relatively short but wonderful period of functional fatness.

Pack away your skinny jeans and treat yourself to a new wardrobe to take you from belly to babies. You will be able to dust off your favorite jeans in a few months' time but for the duration of your pregnancy don't torment yourself by looking longingly at your former wardrobe.

Try to enjoy your body's changing shape and embrace this opportunity to try new styles. You may have always avoided patterns but now discover your

newly feminine form suits florals. You may even continue a new-found love of polka dots postpartum!

During the second and third trimesters your belly will astonish you by growing significantly, seemingly overnight, so be prepared. It is a good idea to have a couple of items on standby so you don't get caught one morning realizing you can no longer zip up the pants that fit the day before.

At the end of your pregnancy be prepared to get inventive and embrace the inner fashion designer. Your tandem belly may challenge some maternity seams made to deal with one baby not two; snip seams, insert elastic panels, or pin things together with ribbon and brooches.

You may not regain your pre-pregnancy figure immediately, so expect to wear your maternity clothes for a while following the birth.

Trimester by trimester

With all this going on, you may be wondering when—if ever—you will experience a pregnancy bloom. While women and their twins' growth vary a lot, as a rough guide you can expect different things from each trimester:

- **First trimester** Pregnancy symptoms can sometimes be troublesome, but there are usually ways of coping (see pp.32–35).
- **Second trimester** This is when you'll probably get that blooming feeling, so enjoy it.

Even though you'll be bigger than singleton moms-to-be, this can also be a good time to get essential things done.

- **Third trimester** Many women become uncomfortable in late pregnancy. Work and household chores can become impossible, and caring for existing children is a challenge, especially if you have a toddler. Take it as easy as you need to, and remember that your last trimester is likely to be shorter than with just one baby.

Maternity wear

A few well-chosen maternity items can keep you feeling comfortable as you expand. The following items will take you through your pregnancy without breaking the bank. You may not be familiar with elastic waists and stretchy panels, but they will be your old favorites by the end of your pregnancy!

Belly band

This stretchy fabric enables you to wear your regular tops longer by covering your belly as it grows.

Shoes

Your feet may widen, too. What a great excuse to go shoe shopping! Think flat, comfortable, and pretty.

Bra

Get measured regularly and choose a nonwired style that is comfortable to wear.

Jeans

Maternity jeans either have elastic panels on the sides or the front. See what suits you best.

Maternity tank

Super stretchy and extra long, these can be usefully layered under tops and dresses.

Leggings

Elastic waistbands are your new best friends, so you can breathe easy as you expand!

Weighty matters

It's not just your uterus getting bigger; the rest of you is, too. In addition to the babies, their placentas, and all that amniotic fluid, you're also adding to your breast tissue and the fat reserves on your hips, thighs, and elsewhere. On the whole, you can therefore expect to gain much more weight than in a singleton pregnancy.

All women vary, but carrying one baby you might put on a modest total of 28 lb (13 kg) in nine months. With twins, you could gain between 40 and 50 lb (18 and 23 kg) or more—the equivalent of a fully loaded vacation suitcase.

The ideal weight change depends primarily on your pre-pregnancy weight. However, it's considered a good thing to put on the pounds early on with twins ("24 lb by 24 weeks" as the saying goes) since that's when the babies are developing most rapidly.

Size and shape

The differences are most obvious when compared with pregnant friends, or with your previous singleton pregnancies.

Your uterus will rise up above the pelvis in the first three months. By the time you're 12 weeks pregnant, your bulge is likely to be the size of a 16-week singleton belly.

From then on, the top of the uterus (called the fundus) tends to be around 4 in (10 cm) higher than with one baby. In addition to your belly being bigger, you may find it's a different shape, with a bit of a bulge toward the sides, too.

By 20 weeks, you could look very pregnant, and by 28 weeks you may look as if you're about to deliver at any moment. Even then, you should go on growing. You might not welcome being this size, but

Changing shape You may start showing sooner than you expected, and your belly can grow in leaps and bounds.

it can be useful for getting a seat on a crowded bus! You might as well sit down when you can, since you may feel tired. But exercise has benefits despite your increasing size (see p.16–19).

Your breasts, heart, and lungs

The changes in your middle are the most obvious of all, as you'd expect. Here's what else is going on during these vital months.

Breasts You've got more hormones on board with a twin pregnancy. One result is that your breasts become warmer and extra sensitive early in pregnancy, and they start getting bigger, too. From around 15–16 weeks the nipples and surrounding skin become darker, and the small bumps around each nipple (called Montgomery's tubercles) enlarge.

By three months you will almost certainly need a new bra (see p.21). Make sure it fits and is comfortable, especially if your breasts feel heavy or painful. Be ready to upsize every month or two. You don't need a nursing bra yet, just a supportive one with wide straps to support the extra weight.

Heart and circulation Less obvious organs are under pressure as well. The volume of your blood actually increases in the first trimester, and even more so in the second trimester. With twins, your blood volume is about twice as great at term as it was before pregnancy.

To cope with this, your heart needs to pump that much harder, and so your heart rate tends to rise. These changes aren't a problem for most women, but they can be a strain on those who already have heart trouble.

Lungs/breathing Shortness of breath is common after 20 weeks. This can be the effect of the changes in the heart and circulation. Anemia is also a possibility, because making two babies uses up more of your vital supplies of iron and folic acid. Routine blood tests will show whether you need extra iron. You won't inevitably become anemic, so supplements aren't routine. As you edge toward your due date, space restriction also plays a part. With such a big belly, there's less room for your lungs to expand fully.

Doctor's advice

Sex

You can usually continue to have sex during pregnancy, as long as you don't have any bleeding or any other problems. If you're in doubt, ask your doctor. Far from being embarrassed by your question, obstetricians are entirely used to the concept of their patients having a sex life!

Later on, as your due date approaches, your babies can literally come between you, and your belly may feel a little unwieldy for anything too active. Even finding a comfortable position for sex can be a challenge. Going on top may seem too strenuous, but lying on your back can be difficult since this will put a lot of weight on your major blood vessels and could make you feel faint. Try side-to-side positions instead, and use pillows to prop up your belly if it feels unsupported. And, if this is your first pregnancy, feel free to be as vocal as you like in bed! Once their babies are born, some parents feel a little inhibited in the bedroom, so make the most of this time. If it all becomes too much of a big deal, keep in mind that you don't need to have penetrative sex to get intimate with your partner and show that you care.

Your developing babies

Inside that expanding belly there is a lot going on, and it starts long
before you know there's a baby in there—let alone two babies.

The first trimester (weeks 0–13)

Your babies are officially called "embryos" until nine
weeks, and "fetuses" after that, which is the time
when each placenta forms fully and takes on the
role of supporting growth.

The hearts begin to develop in the fourth week,
each starting off as a simple pulsating tube. Even
though you can't hear the heartbeats for ages,
a scan will show each baby's heart beating at around
150 to 160 beats a minute.

The digestive system forms in a similar way, from
a tubular structure that starts at the mouth and runs
right down to the tail. Over the next few weeks, the
tube expands, turns and twists, becoming a highly
complex digestive tract for each of your twins.

Arms and legs appear as tiny limb buds at around
five weeks. By six weeks each twin has
a primitive spinal cord and a blob at the top end,
which develops into a head over the next few weeks.

By 12 weeks, most of the major organs have
formed, and your babies will have paper-thin, red,
see-through skin. There's still a lot of maturing to
do, especially for the lungs, skin, and brain.

From now on, each baby's sex becomes clearer.
While there are already ovaries or testicles, nothing
is yet visible from outside. After 12 weeks, a swelling
appears in the genital area of boys, and this
eventually becomes a penis. A scan later in
pregnancy may show your babies' genitals clearly,
though it depends on how they're lying at the time.

3D scan This type of scan shows the babies in a more
recognizable form, so their features and their movements
look more "human."

Ultrasound scan The standard 2D scan gives a wealth
of information about your babies and the placentas, and
allows measurements to be taken.

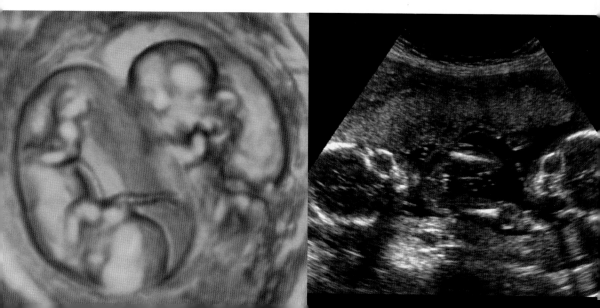

The second trimester (weeks 14–27)

Your babies' faces now look much more human. Eyebrows and eyelashes grow at about 14 weeks, and by 16 weeks the facial bones have formed.

The limbs, too, are well defined by 16 weeks. Your babies already have their own fingerprints, which can be similar but are never exactly the same even if your twins are identical.

Fingernails start appearing around now, although toenails come later. Around the same time, your babies start moving, but you're unlikely to feel anything until 20–22 weeks, when kicks become stronger. By now, muscles are connected with nerves, so movements are also more purposeful.

Each twin's chest moves up and down, making a breathing motion, though your babies get their oxygen through the placenta, not from breathing. At 20 weeks, your babies are covered all over with fine, downy hair called lanugo. This usually disappears just before they are born. Premature babies have more lanugo than full-term babies.

The senses are coming on fast. Your babies can hear from around 15–16 weeks. At 22–24 weeks their eyelids open, but even at 20 weeks they can probably make out light and dark.

The stomach and intestines are already formed and continue to mature. Your twins constantly drink and excrete amniotic fluid. This lets them taste small traces of the foods you eat and may teach them some early likes and dislikes. One theory is that this gives them a taste for your breast milk. The lining of their intestines constantly sheds as the cells renew themselves. (In the next trimester, the waste product this creates becomes dark green and is called meconium—your babies' first poops after being born will be made up of this).

How big are my twins?

Physical growth of each twin is the same as a singleton baby until about 28 weeks, when it tapers off a little.

- At six weeks, each baby is about ⅛ in (4 mm) long from "crown to rump." This is about the size of a small mung bean.
- At 12 weeks, each baby has grown to 2¼ in (6 cm) in length—about the size of a tennis ball, and weighs around ½ oz (14 g).
- By 16 weeks, your babies are about 4 in (10 cm) long (the size of an avocado). Each one weighs around 3½ oz (100 g).
- At the end of 18 weeks, each baby is around 5 in (13 cm) long, and weighs 6½ oz (190 g), or about the weight of a large banana.
- By 20 weeks, each baby is 6 in (15 cm) long,

around the size of a premium mango, and each twin might weigh about 9 oz—over ½ lb (250 g).
- At 22 weeks, babies lie straighter. From now on, their measurements are normally given from head to foot or "crown to heel," rather than crown to rump as before. By now, each could be 11 in (8 cm) long and weigh 15 oz (430 g).
- At 24 weeks, each baby weighs up to 21 oz (600 g) and might be 12 in (30 cm) long from crown to heel.
- At 26 weeks, each baby is likely to be about 14 in (36 cm) long, and weighs 27 oz (760 g).
- By 28 weeks, each baby is about 15 in (38 cm) long, and weighs 31 oz, or almost 2 lb (875 g). There are no reliable growth charts for twins after 28 weeks since growth varies with each pregnancy.

The third trimester (weeks 28–term)

From this point on, growth can vary a lot. On the whole, twins now grow at a slower rate than single babies. Typically, twins are a little lighter than singletons and have less fat, but this isn't always so. There can also be differences between them, with one baby growing more than the other. If this happens in late pregnancy, then your obstetrician might advise delivery soon. When growth diverges in early pregnancy, you may need referral to a maternal-fetal medicine sub-specialist for assessment of the cause and the options.

All being well, however, your twins will be floating happily in separate sacs, taking gulps of amniotic fluid, and listening to the sounds that reach them from outside. They blink, make smiling movements, suck their thumbs, and even grab their own cords. They can hiccup too, as you may notice

Facial expressions As scans show, each baby tries out many facial expressions long before they are born.

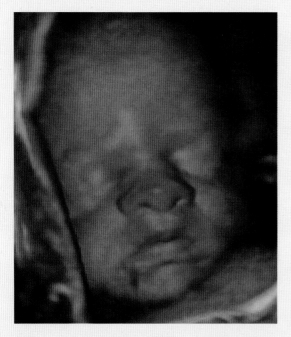

from time to time. This does no harm, but you may find it distracting especially if hiccups occur at night.

From around 32 weeks, space can get a little tight, so your babies may not move quite as freely, but you should still feel frequent movements, especially when you lie down. That's when your abdominal muscles are most relaxed, giving the babies a little extra wiggle room.

There'll be times when one or other twin becomes quiet. Babies sleep in the uterus, and from around 34 weeks they even dream—though what about is anyone's guess.

Interaction in the uterus

It was once thought that babies couldn't do a thing before birth, and had to learn to see, hear, and respond once they left their cosy uterus. Science has now proved that babies are incredibly advanced long before they're ready to be born. Ultrasound shows that before birth twins touch each other, make faces at each other, and, if they're in the same sac, even suck each other's thumbs.

One study shows that twins appear to interact from around 15 weeks, and this reaches a crescendo in late pregnancy. There's little doubt that each baby responds to touch and pressure from the other twin. At 20–22 weeks, around a third of each twin's movements seems to be responses to his or her roommate! But there are also distinct times when even vigorous movement from one twin has absolutely no effect on the other. Presumably this is when one twin is awake and the other is fast asleep.

Whether they actually bond in the uterus is still unknown. Perhaps one day scientists will figure out a way of knowing. Meanwhile, it is hard to believe that close proximity and well-developed senses have no effect at all on your unborn babies.

Size matters As your belly increases, your babies are ever busier getting ready for the big day.

Prenatal appointments and tests

Whether you are carrying one baby or two, the goal of prenatal care is to preempt serious problems and ensure a healthy outcome. And it is usually an amazing experience for you, too.

What's different with twins?

One basic difference is that nobody can see from the overall size of your belly how well each individual baby is doing, so you'll be offered more ultrasounds than if you were pregnant with just one baby. With twins there's also a higher risk of complications. Placenta problems such as placenta previa and preeclampsia (see p.36) are among the most common types of problems.

Of course, this doesn't mean everyone runs into difficulties. Chances are you'll have an uneventful pregnancy, but it still makes sense for doctors to keep a close eye on twin moms-to-be.

If you've already had a baby you probably saw your family doctor, obstetrician, or midwife for regular appointments. This time around, your care will likely by led by an obstetrician, and you may be referred to a maternal-fetal medicine sub-specialist if there are concerns about any complications.

As with any pregnancy, the first step is the initial appointment, which is a long session that goes into medical and social details. This is where you have a chance talk about any personal worries and ask questions, but remember that until you have some tests, you may not get any definite answers.

Soon after this initial appointment, you'll have a vital first ultrasound scan. This scan, done at 11–13 weeks, looks at nuchal translucency, a screening test for Down syndrome. This test is performed on all women pregnant with twins, irrespective of age. The ultrasound also determines whether your twins are a particular kind of identical twin that share just one chorionic membrane (see p.29). This is important for your babies' health and development.

Finding out more Health-care professionals will explain each test to you, and you'll have information pamphlets.

Blood test You can expect several blood tests during your pregnancy. Tell the doctor if these make you anxious.

Monochorionic or dichorionic?

When it comes to how the membranes are arranged around the placenta and babies, there are two basic patterns—monochorionic (MC) and dichorionic (DC). DC twins can be identical or fraternal, but the important thing is that they are no more likely to have complications than any other twins.

About two-thirds of identical twins are MC. They share a placenta and, importantly, have blood vessels that communicate within the placenta, which can lead to unequal blood flow between the babies (see p.37). While this still doesn't mean there'll be complications during pregnancy or labor, MC twin pregnancies deserve extra monitoring. This is even more important for the one percent or so of twins that share an amniotic sac. These are monochorionic monoamniotic (MCMA) twins and sometimes these cords get entangled.

You should know from your first ultrasound whether you have MC or DC twins, and this determines how often your appointments and scans will be. If you have boy-girl twins, your twins aren't identical, so they must be DC.

Prenatal tests

There are three main kinds of prenatal tests:

Routine blood tests First appointment tests include a test for anemia, blood group, sickle cell, and other "hemoglobinopathies" (abnormalities of the red blood cells), also infections such as syphilis, HIV, hepatitis B, toxoplasmosis and chickenpox and rubella immunity. In the second trimester, most women have a glucose challenge test to screen for gestational diabetes.

Ultrasound scans This looks at the space at the back of each baby's neck. It's the only reliable test for Down syndrome in twin pregnancy because blood tests like the maternal serum screen can be

Doctor's advice

Prenatal timetable

This is the basic schedule that many obstetricians have adopted, but there may be differences based on your own circumstances and how your babies progress. Remember that it's your pregnancy, and not one from the pages of a textbook.

For all twin pregnancies
- Early ultrasound at 11–13 weeks.
- Blood pressure and urine testing at 20, 24, and 28 weeks, and then every two weeks.
- Anatomy scan at 18–20 weeks.

For MC twins
- From 16 weeks, scans every two or three weeks.
- Anatomy scan at 18–20 weeks looks at the heart more closely.
- If the babies aren't growing at the same rate, you should be referred to a specialist. Otherwise, delivery is usually planned for the end of the 36th or 37th week.

For DC twins
- Serial ultrasounds at around 24, 28, and 32 weeks, and then every two or four weeks.
- Delivery is usually planned for the end of the 37th to 38th week.

There's always a reason for the examinations and tests that your doctor recommends, which is why it's usually wise to go along with that guidance—but that's not the same as following advice blindly. Throughout your pregnancy you're entitled to ask questions if you have concerns, request any extra information that makes sense to you, and to discuss areas where you don't necessarily agree with what is happening.

misleading when there's more than one baby. It can also detect many other problems. It is also a good measure of your babies' growth, and of how much amniotic fluid there is—and it can tell you your babies' genders, too!

Another ultrasound scan, the anatomy scan, is usually done between 18 and 20 weeks. It lasts around 30–50 minutes and takes a very detailed look at your babies. Don't worry if the ultrasound tech is quiet during some of it, since it requires concentration, but ask for any findings to be shown to you on the screen before you leave.

The ultrasound tech looks carefully at your babies' heads, which can show up certain brain problems. Examining their faces can rule out cleft lip. This scan also checks your babies' limbs, spines, and abdomens, to make sure they are fully formed. The heart and large blood vessels get a particularly close look, especially if you have MC twins. The

ultrasound tech can actually see each of the heart valves open and close rhythmically. The kidneys and urinary system also get the once over, and the tech looks at the placenta and amniotic fluid. The amount of amniotic fluid is important, as is the position of the placentas, though this can change as your pregnancy continues.

Chances are that all will be well. Most moms-to-be leave their ultrasound happy and reassured, and looking forward to meeting their babies. But make sure you ask any questions you need to.

Invasive tests You are unlikely to need these, but you may want to consider amniocentesis or chorionic villus sampling (CVS) if nuchal translucency suggests there might be a problem, or if

Ultrasound scans Ultrasounds give you a first glimpse of your babies, and each scan is a moment for bonding.

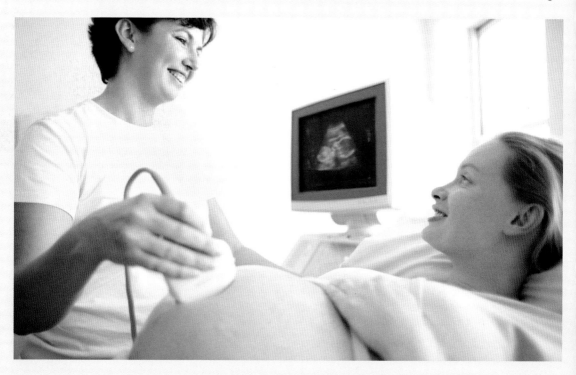

there's some other reason for believing your babies are at high risk (for example, you already have one child with a chromosome disorder). These tests carry some risk to the babies, so they're not routine.

CVS is usually given between 10–13 weeks, but it can be done later. The test samples some of the cells on the edge of the placenta, which are then analyzed to detect chromosome problems (such as Down syndrome, cystic fibrosis, and muscular dystrophy). Because it's a diagnostic test, the result tells you with over 99 percent accuracy whether one of your twins has a particular condition. It also reveals the gender of each baby, but you will be asked if you want to know this.

Amniocentesis is done later in pregnancy, after 15 weeks. The test samples some of the fluid around each twin. The fluid taken contains a few cells from the baby in that sac, so it allows chromosome analysis. With twins, amniocentesis has one

advantage: the specialist can inject dye to be sure each sac was sampled. With CVS, if both samples are identical you may not know if it's because you have identical twins or because the same baby's tissues were sampled twice. Like CVS, amniocentesis is done under ultrasound control to guide the needle safely to its destination.

Most women find prenatal tests reassuring. But before you have any tests, you should really consider what you might do if the results suggest there could be a problem, however unlikely that may be.

Sometimes only one twin has a condition. Should it be your choice to do so, it is often possible to terminate just part of the pregnancy (so called selective termination). In such circumstances, you would have already been referred to a specialist, so you would be able to talk it all through with professionals who have a lot of experience in these very difficult situations.

Ask the parents

Appointments and tests

Not every twin mom-to-be enjoys the intense monitoring schedule planned for her. If you're feeling apprehensive before a scan or checkup, try to think of these additional appointments as a twin perk. Treat each consultation as an opportunity to find out more about what's going on inside your belly. The ultrasounds can be really enjoyable since you can literally see what's happening to your babies as they grow and develop.

At most appointments, you'll have to provide a urine sample to test for protein. Bottles of urine will quickly replace the sanitary protection that you used to carry around in the pocket of your handbag!

Lying down for scans during the later stages of your pregnancy can make you feel queasy because the weight of your belly presses on the large blood vessels within your abdomen. Ask for a pillow to raise your head slightly and try to enjoy the procedure.

Most ultrasound techs are happy to explain what's happening on the scan if you ask, and you can usually get a picture, too. Many scan print-outs fade over time, so photocopy your favorite ones to make sure they last a lifetime.

Whether you're talking to the ultrasound tech or your doctor, ask that any medical terminology to be explained in simple terms and don't feel rushed during your appointments. Write down any questions that you have beforehand to make sure you don't leave without having all your questions answered.

Common symptoms

Some pregnancy symptoms can seem worse when you're having twins, especially the ones caused by a bigger dollop than usual of pregnancy hormones, or the size of your growing belly.

Some pregnancy side effects

You can't expect to grow two new humans in the space of just a few months without having a couple of bumps along the way. Many symptoms come on early then ease off after a few weeks. The reassuring fact is that, as a rule of thumb, the more of these early symptoms you have, the better the babies are growing. Even so, there's usually something you can do to make yourself more comfortable.

Fatigue is an early symptom. It is often no worse in twin pregnancy, but it can be very draining, especially if you are still working or have an older child to care for. There's no easy answer, so just go with the flow and rest when you need to. Fatigue tends to ease up by the second trimester, though you may naturally feel tired again toward the end when you get really big. If you ever find that you're unusually breathless as well, speak to your doctor because you may be anemic.

Headaches, too, tend to occur early on, though not every woman gets them. The symptoms may be a nagging ache around the forehead, with a feeling of fullness, and usually occur due to hormone changes. Headaches usually respond to the occasional dose of acetaminophen. If you get headaches in the second half of pregnancy, it could be a symptom of preeclampsia, which can be dangerous for you as well as your babies (see p.36). See your doctor immediately.

Nausea tends to start early on, often around the first missed period. It's thought to be caused by high

Nausea A ginger cookie can help, though real ginger is more effective and contains less sugar.

levels of the hormone HCG. Often dubbed morning sickness, it can unfortunately last all day for the first three months, especially in a twin pregnancy. Try to avoid spicy and fatty foods. Eat little and often, and make a point of including carbohydrates at each meal. Steer clear of anything that seems to trigger your symptoms, whether it's strong smells or long car trips. Nibbling on a piece of ginger (or ginger cookies) can stave off nausea. In most cases, morning sickness subsides by three months, but if you're vomiting or losing weight, see your doctor for treatment. Some women need a prescription to control nausea and vomiting.

Heartburn can occur anytime in pregnancy. It's due to the hormone progesterone, which relaxes the muscle within the stomach from early in pregnancy. Later on, pressure from your belly comes into play and some of the tips for nausea can relieve heartburn, too. Try sleeping with more pillows and avoid wearing tight clothes. Drink milk to neutralize stomach acid. If simple measures don't help, ask your doctor for antacids. These are safe in pregnancy, as long as you don't have heart trouble or high blood pressure.

Vaginal discharge is normal in early pregnancy. It is due to changes in the vaginal lining, as well as extra blood flow to all of the tissues in the pelvis. See your doctor if it becomes irritating, itchy, or uncomfortable, or if you notice that the discharge is smelly, yellow, green, or blood stained. This may mean an infection, which needs treatment.

Constipation is again a progesterone-linked symptom, because this hormone slows down gut activity. Combat constipation by eating more fruit and vegetables, drinking fluids, and getting regular exercise. Don't take laxatives unless your doctor recommends them since they can be too powerful. Fiber preparations, however, are usually safe and your doctor can prescribe these. Dealing with constipation can also prevent hemorrhoids.

Hemorrhoids are varicose veins around the anus. They don't always cause trouble, but when they do, symptoms can include a lump (or several lumps), pain, itching, and bleeding. You can help prevent hemorrhoids by avoiding straining when you go to the bathroom. If you develop any symptoms, check with your doctor or pharmacist who will recommend a treatment. Most cases get better after the birth, but labor can temporarily make them worse. Afterward, things improve, but it's common to be left with a few skin tags near the anus. These are usually harmless.

Analgesics

Doctor's advice Acetaminophen is considered the safest analgesic in pregnancy, but never exceed the recommended dose. Ibuprofen should not be taken and never take aspirin unless it is prescribed for you. If you're unsure about a medicine, ask your pharmacist if it is suitable during pregnancy. If you're taking a prescription-only drug, don't stop abruptly, but ask your doctor if it's suitable now that you're expecting. Some medications for long-term conditions such as high blood pressure may need to be changed during pregnancy.

Avoid self medication Be careful with herbal remedies, too. Don't assume a product is gentle just because it is natural.

Your pregnancy

Varicose veins aren't inevitable, though they are common, especially if you have a family history of them. They're more common in pregnancy for two reasons: one is high levels of the hormone progesterone, which dilates veins, and the other is that your growing babies put pressure on the deep veins in the pelvis. It helps to put your feet up when sitting down, and to keep moving when you're up and about. Regular walks help stimulate blood flow up the leg. Avoid wearing tight clothing because it can constrict the veins in your thighs and pelvis. You could consider maternity support stockings if you spot any varicose veins. Like most other symptoms, they tend to get better after the babies are born, but they are likely to recur.

Backache is no real surprise when you consider the load on your spine and, as your babies get bigger, on your abdominal muscles. There's also the hormone relaxin, which makes joints a little looser in pregnancy. Watch your posture, wear flat shoes,

avoid heavy lifting, and try to keep active (see pp.16–19). Stretches several times a day can ease an aching back. If you use a computer or sit at a desk for long periods of time, make sure you take regular breaks to stretch. The same applies to long car trips. It's also important to check that your desk and car seat are at the right height for you.

Carpal tunnel syndrome (CTS) is numbness or pain in the hand(s) and is caused when swollen tissues put pressure on the median nerve in the wrist. This nerve controls sensation and movement in part of the hand. In CTS, you can get tingling, numbness, or pain in the thumb, index finger, middle finger, and half the ring finger. Many women report that symptoms are often worse in the morning and most noticeable when trying to do delicate tasks such as sewing. You may find that you have difficulty grasping objects or feel a dull ache in your hand or forearm. The fluid retention common in pregnancy makes CTS more common when you are expecting.

Headache In the first few weeks, headaches are common, but always talk to your doctor about headaches in later pregnancy.

Backache Pain is common as your belly grows and increases in weight but good posture and regular exercise both help when coping with backaches.

Shaking or moving your hand can help and some women sleep with the affected hand up on a pillow, while others find that dangling their hand down is better. If you use a keyboard, take frequent breaks and move your fingers around. Your doctor may be able to demonstrate some stretching and circling exercises to improve your mobility and circulation. Wearing a wrist splint can also help; you can buy one or ask at a pharmacy. Symptoms may last throughout pregnancy but should ease within three months of the birth. A few twin moms-to-be have severe symptoms, and possibly muscle wasting around the thumb. If you have persistent numbness, you may need an injection or even minor surgery to relieve pressure on the nerve.

Pelvic joint pain or pelvic girdle pain is caused by increased movement between the two bones at the front of the pelvis. This joint is called the pubic symphysis and the condition is also known as symphysis pubis dysfunction. Pain can come on during or even after pregnancy because of the increased weight of your growing babies, and also because the hormone relaxin softens the ligaments of the joint, giving the bones extra movement. About 20–25 percent of pregnant women get some form of pelvic pain, and it seems to be more common in those carrying twins. You may notice a clicking sensation or pain upon walking, going upstairs, turning in bed, or getting dressed. If you have pelvic pain symptoms, talk to your doctor. You may need referral to a physical therapist who specializes in dealing with pregnant women. Doing pelvic tilt exercises and improving your posture can help. But you may also need some form of manual therapy to help realign the joint.

It is important to remember that not every twinge is due to your pregnancy, and occasionally there's something else going on. If your symptoms are unusual, contact your doctor.

Ask the parents

Sleep

Moms of multiples can expect sleepless nights once their babies are born, but physical discomfort and anxiety can make it hard to shut down long before the pitter-patter of tiny feet actually arrive.

Finding a comfy position once you have taken your weary self to bed can be hard, especially in the latter stages of pregnancy when your belly is large. V-shaped body pillows can be positioned to support your belly and take the weight off your muscles and spine. If possible, rest during the day, since naps can help alleviate fatigue after a restless night.

Stay hydrated to avoid headaches. If leg cramps keep you awake, try eating bananas to keep them at bay. Warm milk before bedtime can be soothing and also provides you with much-needed calcium.

Sleep Try using pillows to find a position that supports you and is comfortable.

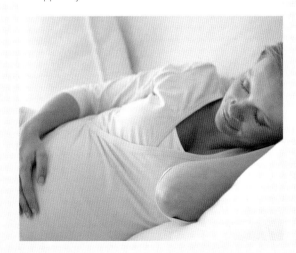

Possible complications

While serious problems are rare in pregnancy, it is wise to know about possible complications. You will be better equipped to look out for early symptoms and to bring up any concerns with your doctor.

Bleeding

This is about three times more common in twin pregnancies, possibly because the placentas occupy a larger part of the uterus surface. Any bleeding is from you, not the babies, but it can be alarming all the same if it happens. Bleeding is most common in the first trimester, though it can occur later, too. In early pregnancy, bleeding is often not serious and may ease, but it can be a sign of miscarriage, so you should always report it to your doctor. It is likely that you'll need to have an ultrasound to make sure your twins are all right.

High blood pressure and preeclampsia

High blood pressure and/or preeclampsia are more common, too, affecting some 15 percent of twin pregnancies. The cause is unknown but it is a problem with the placenta. Trouble usually develops after 20 weeks, with high blood pressure and protein in the urine. The important thing about preeclampsia is that it is linked with poor growth of the babies, possible stillbirth, and problems for the woman, occasionally including convulsions and death.

Spotting preeclampsia early is the main reason for having regular prenatal checkups, but the condition can come on between appointments, and it can develop rapidly. Moreover, not all health-care professionals are well versed in recognizing and dealing with it. Preeclampsia doesn't always cause symptoms but there can be:

- severe headaches, with or without vomiting
- blurred vision, flashing lights
- sudden swelling of hands or face (you can usually

Prenatal checkups High blood pressure is an important sign of potential problems, so your doctor will measure it at every appointment.

ignore mild swelling of feet and ankles or slight tightness of rings)
- pain under the ribs, usually on the right but maybe in the middle
- shortness of breath

If you have any of the above symptoms, see your obstetrician right away for a checkup (leave a urine sample). Bed rest, medication for high blood pressure, and monitoring the pregnancy closely can be enough, but sometimes the best option is to deliver the babies early. If this is in the cards you'll have an injection of steroids to help the babies' lungs deal with arriving before term. After the birth, your blood pressure usually subsides within a few weeks, though in some women that is when it rises for the first time.

Gestational diabetes

This refers to high blood sugar (glucose) in pregnancy, and it happens because hormones from the placenta can block the effect of insulin. You may feel very thirsty or hungry, and urinate (even) more often. Fatigue and blurred vision are other possible symptoms. But on the other hand, you may have no signs at all, so urine is regularly checked for glucose during pregnancy. If a routine test shows glucose, you may need to have further blood tests after a sugar load (glucose tolerance test) to confirm the diagnosis. The treatment of diabetes in pregnancy is the same as for any type of diabetes. The good news is that it usually clears up after the birth.

Twin-to-twin transfusion syndrome (TTTS)

This is a serious complication that affects some MC pregnancies (see p.29). It is due to the communicating blood vessels in the placenta, so the twins share their circulation. In TTTS, one baby gets much more blood than the other. The twin who gets less blood can become small and anemic, while the other one grows larger but can suffer heart failure and produces a lot of amniotic fluid. Symptoms you might notice include a rapidly enlarging belly from hydramnios (excess amniotic fluid). You may also become short of breath.

There are treatments for TTTS, including laser therapy to deal with the blood vessel cross-channels that cause the problem. You may need to be referred to a specialist for assessment and treatment, so the sooner you tell your doctor about your symptoms, the earlier your babies can get vital help.

Ask the parents

Voice your concerns

The same advice applies to any other worrying symptoms you may get during pregnancy. Of course you will experience a degree of discomfort and an assortment of "complaints" during pregnancy, especially when you are carrying more than one baby, but the chances are that those twinges and aches will simply be due to the dramatic changes taking place in your body and its response to your growing babies. For your own peace of mind, however, always tell your doctor promptly about your worries, and make sure they hear you. And if anything sudden or painful occurs see your doctor without delay.

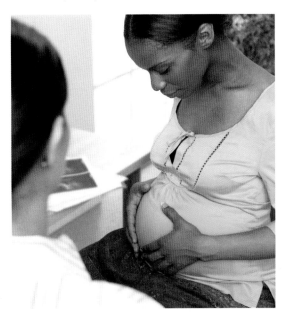

Know your options Before you decide on what course of action best suits you, get to know all the options you have.

Preparing for your babies' arrival

Your hospital bag

Twins often arrive early, so have your bag packed from 26 weeks. Include your partner in the packing process so they can find items when you ask for them!

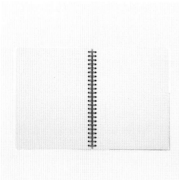

✴ Your birth plan

Take a spare copy in case there are shift changes during your labor and the original goes missing.

✴ Nursing bras

It is worth investing in a couple of well-fitting nursing bras so that you can wash-one/wear-one.

✴ Maternity pads and breast pads

Pack one pack of each for bleeding and any milk leakage after birth.

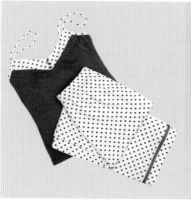

✴ Wash bag

Remember your toothbrush and toothpaste, lip balm, shampoo, hair bands, deodorant, and wet wipes.

✴ Pajamas

Soft stretchy cotton is ideal for breast-feeding and will be easier on a cesarean scar if you have one.

✴ Comfortable panties

You can buy disposable briefs, but you may feel tender, so big cotton panties will be most comfortable.

Your babies' hospital bag

Keep your babies' bag packed from 26 weeks, too. During the last few days it will be a comforting reminder of what your waddling is in aid of!

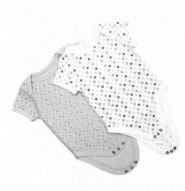

✴ 12 onesies

Short-sleeved onesies are easier to put on and take off and can be worn under a sleep suit.

✴ 12 sleep suits

The ones with snaps all the way down the front are the easiest to put on and take off.

✴ Two hats

Compared with your uterus, the hospital is comparatively chilly, so hats will help prevent heat loss.

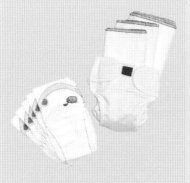

✴ Six burp cloths

Babies can often bring up milk after feedings so it is useful to have a burp cloth on hand.

✴ Package of diapers

Choose either disposable or cloth diapers, and remember to pack enough for two babies.

✴ Two blankets

Don't forget soft light blankets to keep your babies warm when you take them home.

What to buy

You will not need two of everything, but making the right choices about equipment and products will help your new family get off to the best start.

Strollers

Side by side, one in front of the other, three wheels, or four? You may not have as much choice as singletons with regard to your stroller, but there are still several styles to consider.

Tandem strollers are more streamlined and lightweight. Many have attachments that modify them to suit your babies' changing needs. Although more expensive, designs that grow with your babies can be more cost effective in the long run. It is worth investing in this essential piece of gear.

Your lifestyle (and doorway size) will influence your choice, but consider whether you would like your babies to face you or the big wide world? Would you like your babies to lie completely flat? Do you need heavier duty all-terrain tires? Will the stroller fit in your car when folded? If you drive your twins from A to B, consider a travel system with car seats that can be clipped onto the stroller frame.

Ask moms at your local mommy group what stroller or travel system they "drive" and if they would recommend it. It's useful to have your travel system arranged before you bring your new family home from the hospital so that you and the babies are mobile from the start. Twins are often premature, so consider making your stroller one of your first purchases so you can get familiar with how it works and be confident when it comes time to use it.

Car seats

For the safety of your babies, ensure that you know how to correctly install the car seats. Initially, your

Tandem stroller You may worry about the size but tandem strollers are stylish and maneuverable.

babies will need rear-facing seats, until they have outgrown the seats' height/weight limit at around 22 lb (10 kg). Practice installing the car seats when they are empty because it is easier to get familiar with your equipment before you add babies!

LATCH or UAS car seats attach securely to installed connectors in the structure of the car; you can check if this format is compatible with your vehicle. Alternatively, the car seat belt is used to attach the chair to the car. Either way, check the manufacturer's instructions to ensure you install the seats safely and securely.

Never be tempted to hold your babies on your lap in the car—it is not safe and they will be very vulnerable if you were to have an accident.

Cribs

Your babies may share everything from onesies to bath water and even a nursery, but after three months, when your babies start rolling over and are more likely to disturb each other, they will each need a crib. You may, of course, choose to put them in individual cribs from day one.

Cribs with a drop side are not recommended due to recent safety recalls in Canada. Consider investing in cribs that can be made into beds. If you buy used, make sure that you purchase new mattresses.

You will need mattress protectors and fitted cotton sheets. It is a good idea to have spare sheets so that you always have clean, dry ones available. You may also want to buy large burp cloths for swaddling and tucking in. When they are a little bigger, consider baby sleeping bags. These can help your babies sleep longer because they cannot wiggle out of them! Make sure babies are always placed in their cribs in the feet-to-foot position.

A practical and safe nursery

It is a good idea to install a changing station in the nursery, and elsewhere in the house. You don't need a table, but set aside space in your home where you can change your babies. You will need a mat, wipes or warm water and cotton pads, diaper cream, diapers, and a place to dispose of them.

A night-light or dimmer switch will enable you to check on your babies without waking them. You will also need a baby monitor so that you can hear them when you are elsewhere in the house.

It is recommended that you and your babies sleep in the same room until they are six months old. Space may determine that this is not possible with twins, so always use your baby monitor.

A nursing chair in the nursery will help you do night feedings with the minimum of disturbance. If you keep the nursery quiet and dark, it will help your babies to learn the difference between night and day. Black-out blinds can be useful for keeping the room as dark as possible.

You might want to plan your nursery fairly early on in your pregnancy, since twins often arrive sooner so it is a good idea to be prepared. Make sure that your nursery is easy to clean; carpet and rugs can harbor dust mites so consider hardwood floors or vacuum regularly.

Remember your nursery has to be safe as well as stylish! Do not put pillows, comforters, thick bedding, bumper pads, or toys in the cribs, and make sure there are no cables, cords, strings, or other items that could pose strangulation or choke risks for your babies.

Feet to foot Tuck in covers and ensure your baby's feet are at the foot of the crib to keep her from slipping under.

Around the house

Your babies' nursery may have been the focus for you while pregnant, but once the twins arrive, you will also be spending time in other areas of the house. There are some items that can help the three of you get organized wherever you are.

Cushions V-shaped cushions can help you get comfortable during the later stages of your pregnancy and are also helpful for breast-feeding. Insufficient support can leave you with poor posture, leading to avoidable aches and pains.

Specially designed cushions help raise your babies to the correct level so that their mouths are in line with your nipples. You will still need to use your hands to cradle your twins' heads but your forearms will also be supported by the cushion so your neck and shoulders can stay relaxed.

You can of course arrange several ordinary cushions to suit you and your babies, but they can slip mid feeding. Breast-feeding twins is not easy, so consider investing in a specially designed pillow.

Bouncy chairs These are incredibly useful—and portable. Buy two chairs and consider styles that have a detachable bar for toys.

You must never leave your babies unattended but the chairs can help liberate your hands so that you can eat a meal or have a well-deserved cup of coffee. Even if your babies become agitated, they can often be soothed by jiggling the chair with your foot, buying you some precious minutes.

As your twins become increasingly mobile, the chairs are a great way of ensuring that twin one can't get into mischief while you tend to twin two.

When your babies can support their heads and necks, you can place them in their chairs to feed them if you are using a bottle. Of course, both you and your babies will enjoy the cuddling that you can share while feeding them in your arms, but

the chairs are useful backup for days when that may not be possible.

Bouncy chairs can also be helpful for sitting your babies in when you start to introduce solid foods, before you move them into high chairs.

Babies love to watch you, whatever it is you are up to, so place them in their bouncy chairs while you do household chores.

Bathing and cleaning Initially, you might like to simply sponge bathe your babies. You can do this at your changing station. You will need two bowls and some cotton pads. Use one bowl for faces and another for bottoms. Use fresh water and cotton pads for each baby.

When you are ready to give your little ones a real bath, you do not need to buy a baby bath or bath seat, but you may initially feel more confident with the aid of a support. Speak to moms of other twins to see what they recommend. A bath thermometer, baby nail scissors, gentle baby bath/shampoo, and hooded towels are all useful, too.

Feeding If you intend to bottle-feed, you will need bottles, nipples, a bottle brush, and sterilizer. You will also need this equipment, as well as a pump, if you would like to express your breast milk. You can store expressed milk in the fridge or freezer in breast milk bags.

Consider buying a notebook and logging feeding times and amounts for each twin. This might sound like unnecessary work but sleep deprivation can muddle your memory and trying to recall who was fed last, how much, what time, and from which breast can be stressful. A quick at-a-glance reference will give you confidence in the early weeks while you adjust to your new role.

Comfortable and content Bouncy chairs allow your babies a view of you and the world around them.

Childbirth classes

There is a range of childbirth classes available, and all aim to help prepare you for labor, birth, and early parenthood. The support gained and friendships made during coffee breaks are equally valuable.

About the classes

Classes are usually booked in accordance with your due date, but given that premature labor is more likely in a twin pregnancy and you may not feel very comfortable or mobile later in your pregnancy, ask if you can join earlier than singletons.

As a multiple mom you may be a minority, but make sure your questions are answered and don't be afraid to ask "How will it be different for me?" Most childbirth classes will cover the following:

- information about labor and birth, including breathing and positions you might want to try.
- explanation of medical procedures and terms, including pain-relief options.
- advice about cesarean sections.
- stress management and relaxation techniques, including massage and breathing work.
- breast-feeding.
- lifestyle changes, both physical and emotional.

For many women, childbirth classes are worthwhile because they provide an opportunity to "ask an expert" and meet other women going through the same thing.

Most hospitals offer childbirth or Lamaze classes to women planning to deliver babies at that hospital (some classes are free, others have a fee). There are also classes run by individual instructors and local groups such as community centers and the YWCA.

New babies and new friends Lifelong friendships are often made at childbirth classes where women can share their experiences of pregnancy and motherhood with others going through it at the same time.

Finding the time

Your employer may allow you time off work, within reason, to attend childbirth classes. However, if you are self-employed or don't want to step away from your job before your maternity leave, then evening classes or one-day courses may suit you better.

You may want to attend more than one type of class or, if you do not want to sign up for a full course, consider half-day workshops. Twins groups and some hospitals run workshops specifically for moms expecting multiples, which are very valuable and informative. The internet is a good way to find what is available in your area, as are other twin moms.

If this is not your first pregnancy, diaper-changing may be familiar territory, but you may still get something out of childbirth classes, not least of all a support network of women having babies at a similar time to you. If you have not had twins before, you may have specific concerns and questions that can be addressed, helping you to feel more prepared. Twin moms who attended the class sometimes return with their babies, and seeing them in action can be a reassuring insight into your future and life beyond the protruding belly.

Classes A great place to meet new mommy friends, acquire knowledge, and ask questions.

Ask the parents

Research your options and see what suits you
You may also want to research other choices of classes, and there are many options available.

The two most popular classes given for techniques used to deal with labor and delivery are Lamaze and the Bradley Method. Parenting classes teach you practical skills for use once your babies are born. Here you can learn to bathe and change a baby by practicing on a doll.

Some classes are primarily for you as the mother, and address questions relating to your physical and emotional journey from pregnancy to birth and beyond. Other classes address you and your partner as a team such as Lamaze and the Bradley Method. In these type of classes, your partner will be expected to participate and should leave equipped with the skills to help you on your big day of twin birth. Going to classes together is a good way for you to feel supported and your partner to feel included.

Emotional preparation

Women expecting just one baby may feel overwhelmed at the prospect of what lies ahead, so with two babies in your belly, you are perfectly entitled to feel a little apprehensive, too.

Shock, panic, and privilege

Becoming a twin mom is a journey that may take you from feeling shocked, to panicked, to privileged. Don't be afraid to voice your concerns and fears to a friend, family member, or doctor. Sometimes just sharing your worries can help you feel better.

It is OK to admit that you feel overwhelmed and worried about how you will manage. It can be helpful to join a twins group to speak to other moms who have no doubt felt much the same as you do.

Positive planning

Writing a birth plan (see pp.58–59) can help you come to terms with your twin mom status. Detailing the birth experience you would like can help you to retain a sense of control and positivity. However, try to stay flexible; doctors may deviate from your plan for the well-being of you and your babies.

Facing your fears

Twins are often born early and may need to spend some time in the Neonatal Intensive Care Unit (see pp.88–89). Staff will be supportive and sympathetic, but it can be distressing if your babies need medical attention so you might want to visit the unit while pregnant to see what happens. Reducing fear of the unknown can help you feel less apprehensive if your babies do need to spend some time there after birth.

Acknowledge the concerns of your existing family

Having a baby can strain even the most robust relationship, and twins come with added pressure.

Birth plan A birth plan is a good way for you to think over how you'd like your labor and delivery to go and it will make you feel mentally prepared as well.

Organize help in advance so you know you won't be on your own immediately following the birth. Recognize the importance of communication and start your journey as twin parents as a team.

Acknowledge that your pregnancy and new additions to the family will affect everyone in your household. Ensure that older siblings play a role in the process in an age-appropriate manner so that they continue to feel loved and included.

Dealing with unwanted attention

Life with a twin-sized belly will give you an indication of the attention your babies will attract once they are born. Twin admiration is good for morale, but it can be exhausting answering the same questions from well-meaning strangers. A simple "thank you for admiring my babies, but we must be on our way" might help you escape their clutches.

Joining the club

It's not all double trouble! There are advantages to having multiples: buy-one-get-one-free offers at the supermarket are pay back for your unexpected buy-one-get-one-free pregnancy. You won't be bombarded with questions about when you are having another one either, because the assumption will be you've completed your family in one belly.

You have membership to the multiple mom club where you can confess all your trials and tribulations safe in the knowledge you will be understood. You have one school run, two smiles, and two goodnight hugs. It doesn't get better than that.

Emotional support Share your concerns with people whose support and understanding you can count on.

Doctor's advice

Get the support you need

Every woman is different, and you can't expect to have exactly the same emotions as other pregnant women. If you're feeling low or worried, don't bottle it up. Chances are there's someone, somewhere who can help you. As a first resort, try your obstetrician. She can support you, or refer you for a short course of counseling if needed.

If there are alcohol or drug issues in your household, you may find it helpful to get in touch with organizations such as Al-Anon. Social services can assist if you're facing difficult domestic circumstances. You can go directly yourself, or your doctor can make arrangements for you.

Many moms-to-be are ambivalent about having twins and have concerns about how they will adjust. It's unusual to go through pregnancy without a single negative thought about work, finances, or lifestyle. While your doctor can give you support, at times there's no substitute for talking to someone friendly who's also had twins. Contact Multiple Births Canada for help with finding a local support group, who can offer confidential listening and support. Just don't ignore any emotional challenges: it's better to face them now.

Pregnancy and work

How long you continue to work while pregnant will depend on your profession and your pregnancy. You may need to make some changes to your working day for the safety and well-being of you and your babies.

Know the risks

It is safe for multiple moms to continue to work while pregnant in many professions, but there are some jobs that may put you and your babies' health at risk. If you have concerns about exposure to the following at work, speak with your employer, who is legally obligated to find you an alternative job if it is not safe for you to continue with your existing responsibilities.

Animals If you work with animals you may be exposed to toxoplasmosis, E. coli, and other disease-causing organisms in their waste or on their bodies.

Food If you handle raw meat you may be at risk of contracting salmonella, E. coli, and listeria.

Chemicals Check the safety data on all chemicals encountered; some are unsafe for pregnant women.

Viral hazards Medical and child-care professions may expose you to viruses and childhood diseases that could be harmful to your unborn babies.

Radiation Repeat exposure to X-rays and other forms of radiation are detrimental to the health of your babies.

Safety first

The environment in which you work needs to be safe for you and your babies. Make sure that there are no trip hazards or slippery floors, and that you are not required to lift heavy items. If you are concerned, speak to your employer and/or your doctor.

Pregnant and professional

Being organized can help you to stay professional throughout your pregnancy. Keep a note of the progress of ongoing projects in case you have to hand them in early. It is important to avoid stress while pregnant, but don't demand special treatment and try to keep up to date with your work.

Staying energized

You are likely to feel most tired during the first and last trimesters. Make sure you stay well hydrated and eat small, regular snacks of nutritious, slow-release foods to keep your energy levels constant.

Thirsty work Keep a glass of water near you at work to remind you to stay hydrated.

If you have a desk job, some simple chair-based stretching exercises can raise your comfort and energy levels and prevent swelling, a common pregnancy complaint (see p.18). Circle your shoulders and wrists, and raise one leg at a time to rotate your ankles.

Elevate your feet by resting them on a footstool to keep puffy ankles at bay and avoid prolonged periods of sitting or standing. Take regular short breaks to stretch your legs and get some fresh air.

Maternity leave and benefits

There are two types of leave available to new parents that will give you job-protected, unpaid time off work. Both are regulated by your provincial or territorial government, so the amount of time that you are eligible for will depend on where you live and your job history. Maternity leave is available for birth mothers only, and ranges from 15–18 weeks. Parental leave can be taken by either parent (or shared between them) and ranges from 12–52 weeks. Your employer is not required to pay you, but some of them do.

You may also be entitled to receive benefits that will pay you a percentage of your regular wage while you are on leave. Benefits are provided by the federal Employment Insurance Act (EI)—you are eligible if you have worked a set number of hours and have been contributing to the EI program. Eligible birth mothers are entitled to a maximum of 15 weeks of paid maternity benefits. Parental benefits of up to 35 weeks are also available for either eligible parent and can be shared between them. Some employers have a benefit plan that will "top up" this amount.

Instead of EI, residents of Quebec are covered by the Quebec Parental Insurance Plan (QPIP); speak to your human resources department about your specific situation.

A healthy balance It is important to get the work/life balance right while pregnant. Take regular breaks during the day and relax once your day is done.

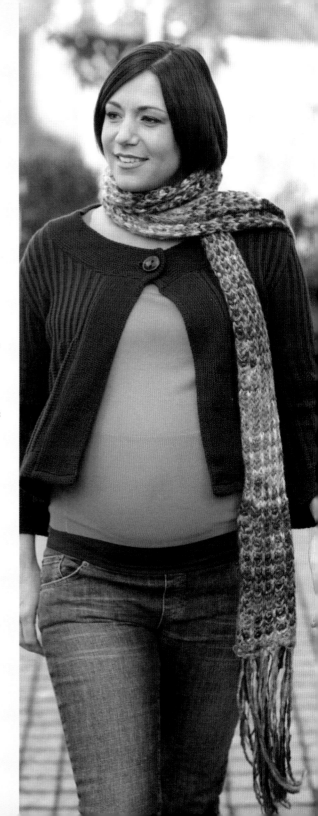

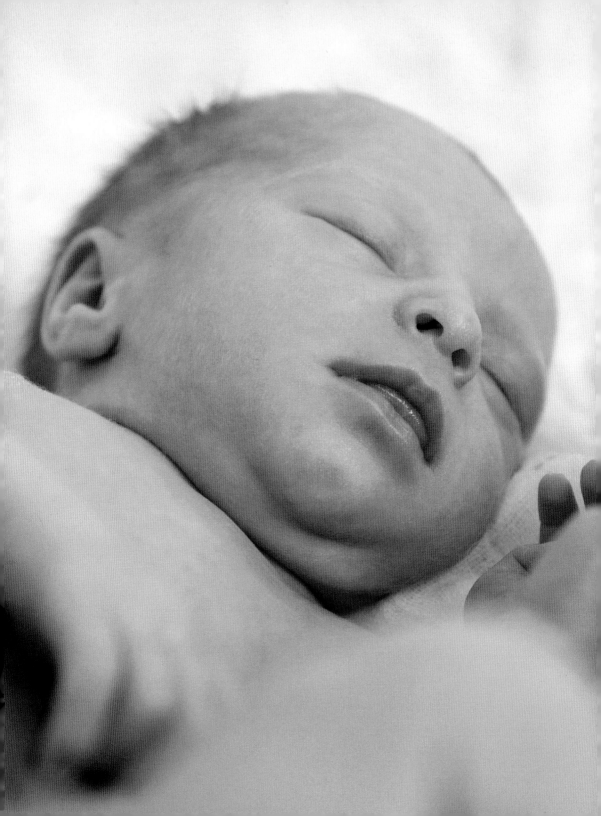

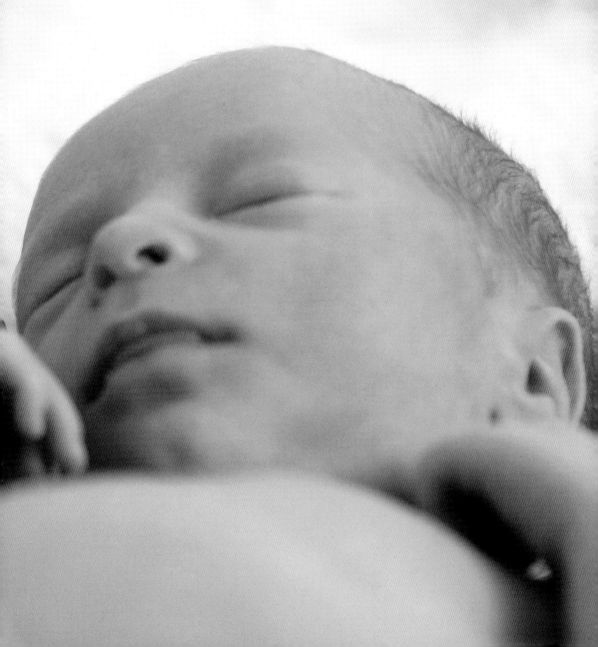

Labor and birth

Birth: the lowdown

You're looking forward to finally meeting your babies, whenever that moment might be, but first here are a few facts about birth that you might want to know before the big day.

When will I give birth?

You've got your due date. In fact it's probably been branded onto your brain since early pregnancy, but that doesn't mean your twins will appear on schedule. Even with a singleton pregnancy, the estimated due date (or EDD) is exactly that—just an expected date of delivery, with about half arriving ahead of time and half afterward. With twins, EDD estimates are even more likely to go out of the window, because twins are prone to arriving early since they compete for space and nourishment. Even so, twins can be slowpokes at the birth game, and there's really no telling if they'll be early or late.

Nesting instinct You may get the urge to clean or organize your home just before going into labor.

Symptoms of labor

It's worthwhile being familiar with the possible signs of labor, even if you know ahead of time that you'll be having a cesarean. Here's what can happen toward your due date.

Nesting As with any pregnancy, "nesting" behavior can start a day or two before labor. You may get a burst of energy and find yourself tidying your home, even cleaning the curtains and wanting to dust the shelves. Not every woman experiences this but it can be very noticeable. Unfortunately, nesting isn't reliable enough to be a useful sign of labor.

Labor Contractions may be mild and irregular at first, before building up in intensity and frequency.

The "show" As pregnancy draws to a close, the cervix starts to soften and dilate. Until then, a plug of mucus protects the precious contents of your uterus, but the changes in the cervix loosen the plug. You'll see a "show"—a discharge of pink or blood-stained mucus that looks like a blob of jelly. Again, not every woman notices a show, and it can occur up to 10 days before labor begins. If you get heavier bleeding, however, you should seek medical help immediately. It is unlikely at this stage in the proceedings, but it may happen, and blood loss can be severe, especially with twin pregnancy. As always, the blood comes from you, not from your babies, but it is still significant and needs to be taken seriously.

Contractions These are the best sign of labor, especially if each lasts more than 40 seconds and they're about three minutes apart. But labor usually starts gradually, and can begin with irregular pain-free contractions called Braxton-Hicks contractions. Once you get noticeable or painful contractions, you should contact your obstetrician for advice. With twins, it's best to do this before you get to the stage of three contractions in 10 minutes.

Water breaking This refers to a release of amniotic fluid when the membranes rupture, and it can be the first sign of labor, or happen much later on when you are already in the hospital. The water can be a sudden dramatic gush that leaves you in no doubt as to what happened, or just a faint trickle that makes you wonder if you coughed and leaked a drop of urine. Either way, it's significant. Put on a sanitary pad and go to the hospital right away. The staff will be able to test if it's urine or amniotic fluid. They will also check your babies' heartbeats and the condition of your cervix.

Don't delay If you feel noticeable contractions or your water breaks, contact your obstetrician right away.

There are two main reasons why you should act right away if your water breaks. One is that it can allow a baby's umbilical cord to fall or "prolapse" into the cervix. Cord prolapse is a rare event, but it is a bit more common with twins, especially when the first twin is breech. It is potentially devastating for that baby since the umbilical cord is compressed, blocking the flow of vital blood. The second reason is that membrane rupture can be an entry route for bacteria. While this is a slightly less urgent cause for concern, doctors often advise delivery within 24 hours of membrane rupture to prevent infection from harming your babies. Alternatively, you may be kept in the hospital for a while for observation. Either way, you should go to the hospital immediately if you suspect your water has broken.

Labor and birth

Other symptoms of labor

Women can experience other signs, too. Every labor is individual, and the way it unfolds depends on your babies' positions and your own unique characteristics as well.

Backache Every woman experiences labor differently, and the early stages and warning signs can vary. The pressure on your pelvis and nerves can give you a backache, or make you want to urinate. As a result, it can be hard to walk anywhere, except maybe to the bathroom. And that backache can persist as labor continues.

Emotions You may feel tired or energized, nauseated or hungry, or just tense and anxious. Try to relax if you possibly can, since being tense tends to make labor harder to deal with, and can even delay the birth itself. Of course, a touch of emotion is understandable at this point. There's still the rest of labor to go through, and once it is all over you will finally meet two very special little people.

The stages of labor

There are three stages in any normal labor.
- The first stage is dilatation of the cervix.
- The second stage is the delivery of the baby's head (quickly followed by the rest of the body).
- The third stage is delivery of the placenta.

During the first stage your cervix changes from a tiny opening to a capacious one that's 4 in (10 cm) in diameter. It's the muscles of the uterus that do all the work here, with every contraction contributing to your progress. One rule of thumb is that the cervix dilates at around ½ in (1 cm) an hour, but this estimate is a little misleading, especially with twins. The cervix can dilate very slowly at first and speed up later—or it can be the other way around. That's why it's not a good idea to expect labor to proceed like clockwork.

How labor differs with twins

If you're having twins, you still only have one first stage. But as you might imagine there are two second stages, one for each twin. Twins are usually a little smaller than singletons, so this part of labor

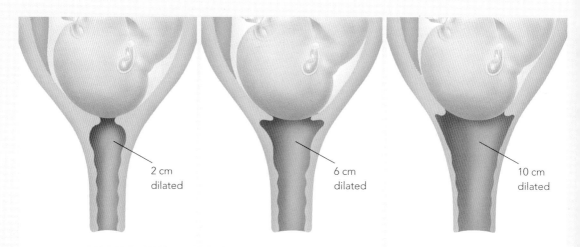

2 cm dilated	6 cm dilated	10 cm dilated

Early labor Contractions may be irregular, but each one helps the cervix thin out and open.

Active labor You're in established labor, with regular contractions that can now move things on quickly.

End of first stage You are now fully dilated, and can soon begin to push the first twin out.

can actually seem easier and quicker than with a singleton. However, the babies can get stressed more easily by the birth, especially if they are premature. And, while the first twin is born, the second twin has to put up with all of the contractions that are pushing the first one out.

The delivery of the placentas is not much different with twins, except that there are often two of them. They usually come out after both babies are born (see p.69).

Your delivery

These stages of labor only apply if you have a vaginal birth (see pp.68–69). Half of all twins are delivered this way, with the other half arriving by cesarean (C-section) as this is deemed safer for many twins, especially monochorionic (MC) twins because of the cross-channels between their circulations (see p.29). As one twin gets squeezed during vaginal birth, blood is diverted to the other twin, with the risk of overloading his or her circulation.

Delivery is obviously something you need to talk about with your doctor, but there's usually no real rush. The method of delivery doesn't necessarily need to be decided until late pregnancy. Current practice is to discuss delivery options at around 34–36 weeks (32–34 weeks if you have MC twins), unless there are other issues, such as placenta previa. At this time, you can also explore some of the options for pain relief.

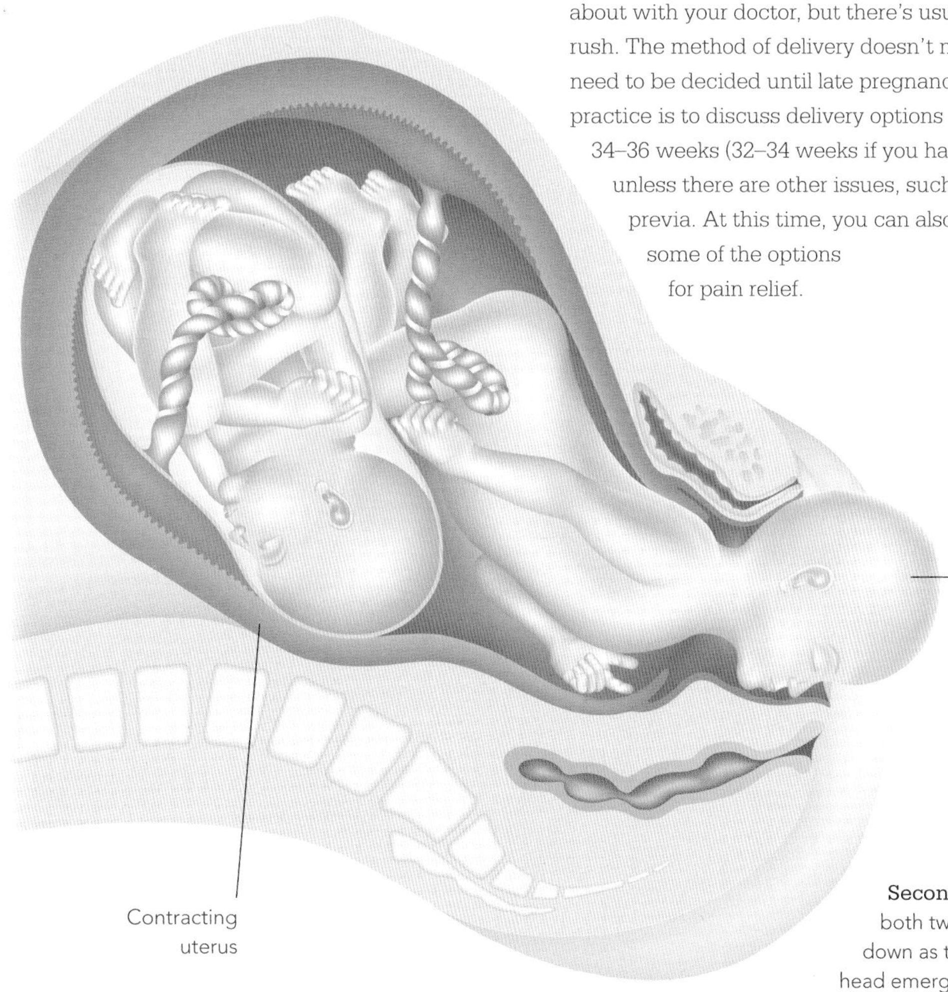

The head crowning

Contracting uterus

Second stage Here both twins are head down as the first baby's head emerges.

Your birth plan

A birth plan details what you would like to happen during labor and birth. Not everyone writes one, but the process of creating a plan can help you come to terms with and prepare for what is to come.

If things don't go according to plan

It is important to remain flexible and try not to be disappointed if your birthing experience cannot follow the plan. Birth is unpredictable and you and your medical team will ultimately want to prioritize the health of your babies.

What goes in to your plan will depend on if you are hoping to have a vaginal birth or cesarean section, but you might like to consider the following:

Vaginal delivery

Your birth plan can include anything that will help make the experience as positive as possible for you, your partner, and your babies. You might want to consider some of the following:

- Who would you like to stay with you during labor and birth—your partner, mother, friend, or other?
- Would you like your birth partner to stay with you all the time?
- What sort of pain relief would you like?
- Would you like a birth ball?
- Would you like to move around if possible?
- Would you be prepared to have your water broken (membranes ruptured)?
- Would you like music?
- Would you prefer to tear naturally or have an episiotomy if necessary?
- Who would you like to cut the cords?
- Would you like to hold your first baby before delivering the second?
- Would you like to hold your babies as soon as they come out or would you like them cleaned and given to your partner first?

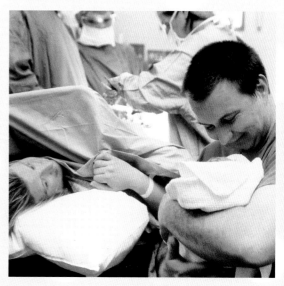

Birth day A life-changing day that has been eagerly anticipated can be enjoyed by both of you.

- Would you like the third stage of delivery managed naturally or have an oxytocin injection?
- Would you like your babies to stay with you unless they need special care?
- Would you like some quiet time as a family if all is well?
- Would you mind having medical students present?

Cesarean birth

Although by definition a cesarean birth will have a higher degree of medical intervention, you can still make your birthing experience personal and special. The following may give you some ideas that you might like to include in your plan:

- Would you like your partner present? If not, who would you like as your birth partner?
- Would you like the screen removed so you can see your babies being lifted out?
- Would you like your babies to be weighed and checked in the delivery room so that, if all is well, they can stay near you?
- Would you like music playing? If so, make a play list and check with the hospital what format you need to have it on so that it can be played during your babies' birth.
- Would you like your voice to be the first your babies hear?
- Would you like photographs?
- Would you like your babies to be cleaned before you hold them?

- Would you like to hold the first baby and then have him/her passed on to your partner so you can hold the second?
- Would you like your partner to hold the babies first?
- Would you like to stay together as a family while you are getting stitches?
- If you have a general anesthesia who would you like to be with the babies until you come around?
- If the babies need some extra help after birth, does the hospital have the appropriate facilities on site or would they need to be transferred elsewhere?
- If possible, would you like to try to breast-feed your babies before you are reunited in the recovery room after you've had your stitches put in?
- Would you like some help establishing breast-feeding?

Vaginal birth plan

Your babies' health must be the priority so try to stay flexible and positive if things don't go according to your plan.

My birth plan

- I appreciate the need for both babies to be closely monitored but would like to be free to move around during labor when possible.
- I would like my partner to stay with me.
- After I have held twin one, pass him/her to my partner while twin two is born.
- I would like a choice of pain relief to be made available. I would like to start with breathing but would like guidance on if/when an epidural might be advisable.
- If possible I would like my babies delivered without the aid of forceps.

Cesarean birth plan

Discuss your plan with your doctor and ask if there is anything else that you should consider, and don't forget to take several copies with you when you go to the hospital.

My birth plan

- We would like to be able to take photos in the delivery room.
- If possible I would like to avoid the use of forceps and prefer the babies to be delivered by hand.
- I would like the babies to be held up right away so I can see them before they are taken away to be cleaned.
- If possible I would like to hold each baby while I am getting stitches so that I can have some physical and eye contact before they are taken to the nursery.

Premature babies

"Full term" is considered to be 37 weeks for twins, since that's when most are at their healthiest. But many twins are born ahead of schedule, and some arrive very early.

Why are twins premature?

Almost 60 percent of twins in Canada are born premature. The reason is often said to be lack of space in the uterus, but if that were the only cause, then every mom with twins would probably deliver around 28 weeks. The real cause is much more likely to be inability of the placenta(s) to keep up with the demands of two growing babies.

There are many possible causes for premature (pre-term) labor, which apply to singleton as well as twin pregnancies. They include vaginal, cervical, or even urinary infection.

Membrane rupture, a baby's health problems, or excess amniotic fluid can trigger labor too. The woman's lifestyle can be a cause, especially if she smokes or uses recreational drugs such as cocaine. For reasons that aren't clear, very young or very mature moms also tend to have premature births.

What your babies may be like if born early

On the bright side, premature twins often mature more quickly than singleton babies of the same age. Twins often survive from around 24 weeks, but a lot depends on the circumstances and there are no

Early arrivals Pre-term babies tend to be smaller and have less fat, but they usually grow well.

hard-and-fast cut-off dates. Obviously, the earlier your twins arrive, the more problems they are likely to face, but not all babies are the same.

Pre-term babies are smaller, and may look very thin from lack of fat under the skin. Their lungs are immature and they may have trouble breathing, especially if born before 34 weeks. But this condition, called respiratory distress syndrome (RDS), can be treated with a ventilator, and with surfactant, a substance that helps lungs expand and take in oxygen.

Premature babies may not have a good sucking reflex. Besides, their digestive systems aren't always ready to process breast milk. They can even develop inflammation of their intestines, though again, there are treatments for this.

Scans show that there can also be some bleeding into a premature baby's brain. Called intraventricular hemorrhage, it's most likely before 32 weeks, but fortunately it isn't always as serious as it sounds.

Arriving before 32 weeks can interrupt blood vessel development. One possible result is called "retinopathy of prematurity," where the eyes don't mature on time. This can resolve on its own, but it sometimes needs laser treatment.

Predicting and preventing premature labor

Unfortunately, it's not possible to predict whose twins will arrive early, which is why you need to know about premature labor and to be ready for it. If you have contractions at any time in pregnancy, or any other symptoms of labor (see pp.54–56), always seek medical advice immediately. Sometimes tests help at this stage, for instance, ultrasound assessment of the shape of your cervix and a vaginal swab to test for the presence of fetal fibronectin (a protein released when labor is on its way).

With pre-term labor, the first step is usually bed rest because it takes the pressure of the babies off

Feet up Rest can help ease early pre-term labor, because it increases blood flow to the babies.

your cervix, and also boosts the blood flow through the placenta. Taking in fluids helps too, because dehydration can trigger contractions.

Then there are various treatments than can stave off full-blown labor. The most common include magnesium sulphate (given intravenously), indomethacin, and nifedipine. While some of them can have side effects, you and your babies will be closely monitored for any unwanted effects. Sometimes side effects can even be good: several pieces of research show that magnesium sulphate helps prevent problems such as cerebral palsy in premature babies. However, for the time being, the evidence isn't strong enough to suggest that everyone should be given this drug.

It's still not clear from scientific studies how much treating premature labor really improves the long-term outcome for the babies, but the really crucial thing is that it helps buy time. If you go into labor early, you will usually get two steroid injections 12 to 24 hours apart, to speed up lung development and prevent RDS.

The hospital environment

Multiple moms require a larger team around them when giving birth, but that doesn't rule out a special and memorable birth experience.

A host of reasons for a hospital birth

Most twin moms choose to have their babies in a hospital because there is access to health-care professionals, specialist services, and a neonatal intensive care unit (NICU) in the event that one or both babies need additional care after birth.

The number of people around you when you give birth will depend on what type of birth you have, but because you have more babies to deliver, you can expect to have more people helping with the birth. Having additional people in the room while you have your babies can sound daunting, but it should be reassuring and add to the excitement of the day.

Twin births are interesting and educational, and some staff and students may want to observe. If this is too much for you and you would rather they were not present, then say so.

Who will be at the birth?

Hospital procedures differ, but you can expect the following people to be present:
- **Obstetrician** A specialist in the care of pregnant women, labor, and delivery.
- **Anesthesiologist** A doctor specializing in pain control.
- **Labor and delivery nurses** Nurses who work with the obstetrician to care for you and your babies.
- **Two pediatricians** Doctors who specialize in babies and infants. There will be one for each baby.
- **Medical students** If you have your babies at a teaching hospital, students may ask if they can observe. You can refuse, but student doctors need to gain experience so that when they qualify they can give the best care to their patients and babies.

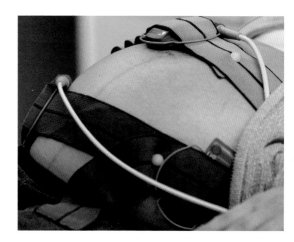

Electronic fetal monitoring At the hospital, your babies' heartbeats may be measured during contractions through electrodes attached to your abdomen.

Two heartbeats, one labor

If you would like to deliver your twins vaginally, both heartbeats will be monitored constantly, either with a strap around your belly for each baby, or with a strap for the second baby and a clip on the first baby's head; this gives a clearer heartbeat reading if it is difficult to find (see p.68–69).

It is important that your hospital team knows the health of both babies at all times throughout labor and birth. If the monitoring equipment suggests that the second twin is having difficulty, they may assist in the delivery of Twin One to speed things up, and either forceps or a vacuum may be used. Otherwise, things will be allowed to continue in their own time.

Once Twin One has been delivered, the cord will be clamped and cut by a nurse or obstetrician, but the placenta usually remains in the uterus until the second baby has been born. You may be able to hold Twin One before Twin Two is delivered.

The position of Twin Two will be checked and the second bag of water may be broken to increase the strength of the contractions. A normal birth should follow. It is unusual for the first twin to be born vaginally and the second one to be born by a cesarean, but it can happen if an urgent delivery is deemed necessary.

There is an increased risk of postpartum hemorrhage in twin births, so the decision is often made to have an active delivery of the placentas. This means that an intramuscular injection (or medication through an IV) is given to make the uterus contract so that the placentas and membranes can be delivered quickly.

No matter how many people are at the birth, once your babies are delivered and declared healthy, you will be left alone to enjoy privacy with your babies.

Cesarean section

If your babies are to be born via a cesarean, you will meet with an anesthesiologist before your surgery. You can discuss pain relief options with him, and he will explain what they are doing at all times. Most women are awake during the surgery and can choose if they want to see the babies being lifted out.

Pediatricians will do initial checkups on both babies when they are delivered and you may be passed your babies almost immediately if there are no problems and you have expressed that you would like this to happen.

If there are no complications, you will be moved to a postpartum ward, your babies will stay near you, and nurses will be on hand to help you. You will be encouraged to get out of bed the day after your surgery, and will likely be able to go home after four days. By the end of the first week, you should be able to do most things for yourself, with help.

Home birth

It can be tempting to want to arrange for a home birth, since many women feel more positive and relaxed about labor in their own familiar environment. You're entitled to your own preference, of course, and there are some midwives who are experienced enough, but the snag with twin births is that things can change very quickly in labor. With good reason, it's said that a 4 in (10 cm) trip through a mother's pelvis is the most hazardous journey any person ever makes, and that's even more true for twins. At home, it's impossible to monitor the babies adequately, have an epidural, or get expert assistance if forceps or a cesarean become necessary. Then there's the possibility of a postpartum bleed for which you might need medical help. Most crucial, you can't get pediatric expertise if it's needed for the babies in a hurry, a fact that convinces the vast majority of moms-to-be into happily opting for a hospital birth.

Labor ward Hospital may be less cosy than home, but it's much safer for twin births.

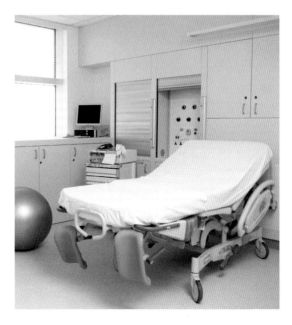

Presentation of twins

You'll often hear health professionals mention the "presentation" of the babies, especially toward the end of your pregnancy. This can have a big affect on how your twins are born.

What is "presentation"?

Presentation, in this context, means how each baby is lying in the uterus. If the pregnancy is straightforward, it's the single most important factor in how your twins will be born.

Your twins are lying in amniotic fluid and moving around, as their kicks will tell you. The amount of amniotic fluid increases until about 32–34 weeks. Production then tails off, but your babies keep growing. That's why the presentation can change

Cephalic If both twins are head down, you're more likely to have a vaginal delivery.

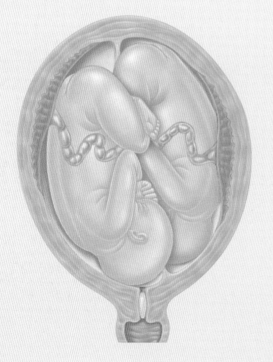

until late in pregnancy, maybe even up to 36 weeks, partly depending on the amount of fluid there is.

If the pregnancy is more complicated, then the presentation at term is less relevant to the method of delivery, since you may bypass labor and have a cesarean (see pp.70–73).

What the different terms mean

Cephalic or vertex (sometimes abbreviated in medical notes to Ceph or Vx) means that the baby is head-down. Breech means bottom-down. Those are the most common presentations, but with two babies, there can be various combinations of cephalic and breech. Twins can also lie in other positions, including transverse (lying across the uterus) and oblique (obliquely or diagonally across the uterus).

How your twins may be lying

In about three-quarters of pregnancies at term, the first twin is head-down (cephalic). In 40 percent or so, both twins are head-down. In 35 percent or so, the first twin is head-down but the second is breech. In about one-quarter of all twin pregnancies, the first twin is breech and the second, breech or cephalic.

Twins lie obliquely or transversely across the uterus in a small fraction of pregnancies. This is more likely if there is a uterus condition such as fibroids. Your babies can also favor unusual positions if you have placenta previa, where one or both placentas lie low in the uterus, interfering with the space available for the babies as well as their exit route. Compared with singletons, twins have less space inside your belly bump.

In a few cases, the way the babies lie can change repeatedly—so-called variable lie. This sometimes rectifies itself toward the very end of pregnancy, but occasionally it can provoke premature labor.

Finding out the presentation

You may have a good idea of your twins' position from the shape of your belly. It tends to be smooth and rounded where a baby's back is. Kicks under the ribs usually mean the baby on that side is head-down. You may even be able to feel or see a foot. If one baby is breech, you may feel a head high up in your belly. Many moms-to-be say that the head feels like a cannon ball. But babies' bottoms can be small, rounded, and hard, too. Even your obstetrician may have trouble figuring out how your babies are presenting. Ultimately, only an ultrasound scan will show the presentation of both babies for sure.

What this means

If both babies are cephalic, there's a good chance that you can try for a vaginal delivery, as long as there aren't any pregnancy complications (see pp.36–37) and no difficulties during labor. If you have a low-lying placenta, you will know about it long before delivery, but it is not always clear until late pregnancy whether it will rule out a vaginal birth.

If the first twin is breech, almost all obstetricians would advise a cesarean, since vaginal delivery is risky. Breech deliveries are possible, but the head is the largest part of a baby and it can take a while to deliver. With a breech baby, the body is by then compressing the cord, cutting off the supply of oxygen. Any delay in the birth of the "after-coming head," as it is called, can therefore be critical.

The tricky call is when Twin One is head-down but Twin Two is breech. Many obstetricians would still consider a vaginal delivery possible, but it depends on the circumstances, such as the size of the babies. If you try for a vaginal delivery, your doctor may turn the second twin during labor to make the birth less hazardous.

In general, there isn't a lot you can do to change your babies' positions. Some advocate various postures, such as going on your hands and knees or leaning forward, but these techniques are most unlikely to work with twins, so there is little point in bothering. Just enjoy your pregnancy.

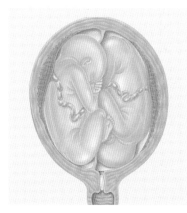

One is breech If the first twin is breech, your doctors will probably advise you to have both babies delivered by elective cesarean.

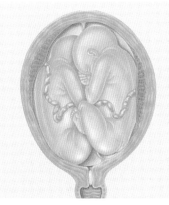

Both are breech Here, too, the breech position makes vaginal delivery difficult so you are most likely to have a cesarean.

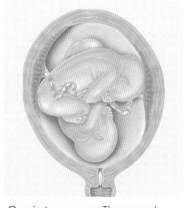

One is transverse The unusual horizontal lie of one twin is likely to lead to a cesarean delivery being recommended.

Pain relief

There are no prizes for giving birth without any drugs, so consider in advance what type of pain relief you would like for your babies' arrival into the world.

What pain relief you are likely to need

Unless you know exactly how your twins will be born, you can't always tell what pain relief will suit you. Every woman is different and you'll have your own preference. Remember though that needs change, especially during labor, so keep an open mind.

The bottom line is that labor tends to be painful. Compared with the size of the pelvis, a baby human's head is far bigger than other species, so don't feel ashamed of wanting something to help you through your twins' birth. Many women hope to do it "on their own." That may sound like a desirable boast to make after the event, but the reality is that pain can make contractions uncoordinated, which slows down labor, and that's not in your babies' interests.

Pain relief options

A relaxation method is well worth practicing, even if you know you'll have a cesarean, since it's a great de-stressing technique after the birth, too. You'll learn more about relaxation at your childbirth class.

Breathing exercises are used by many women to relax and thereby reduce pain. Some women have better results than others but it remains a choice of many women.

TENS (transcutaneous electrical nerve stimulation) uses mild electrical currents to block pain. It's most effective early in labor than in the later stages.

Nitrous oxide, or laughing gas, is inhaled through a hand-held mask which you control. It takes the edge off pain quickly, but can make you feel a bit light-headed or sick.

Strong pain-killing drugs, such as morphine and fentanyl, are still used to reduce pain. But pain relief

takes at least 20 minutes from the time of injection and lasts a few short hours. These injectable drugs have a calming effect which some women like. However, they can also make you (and your babies) less alert and responsive.

Epidurals and spinal blocks offer the most effective pain relief, but need to be done by an anesthesiologist and therefore take some forethought. With an epidural, the anesthesiologist inserts a needle in your lower back and threads

TENS This is most effective in early labor, so you may need another method of pain relief later on.

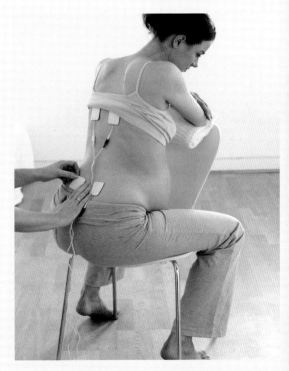

through a very fine tube. This is used to give local anesthetic or even morphine. An epidural takes around 40 minutes to set up and get working. However, since the tube is left in place, there's the option of having more anesthetic later in labor if you need it, for instance, for forceps delivery or a cesarean.

A spinal block is similar but it's a one-time anesthetic injection without a tube. If you have an epidural catheter placed at the same time, it's called a combined spinal-epidural.

Pros and cons of epidurals

With twins, it's worthwhile considering an epidural, even if at first you do not much like the sound of it.

An epidural focuses the pain relief where you need it, it doesn't make you feel drowsy, sick, or out of control, and it won't affect your babies.

Having an epidural does not hurt much and it is suitable for most women. Contrary to popular belief, research shows that it is not linked with an increased risk of a backache afterward. There is, however, a small risk of a headache in a few cases. There is also a small number of cases where an epidural is not 100 percent effective.

For a planned cesarean, an epidural is ideal. But the main benefit with a twin delivery is that the technique is so versatile. If you are in labor and need any intervention, for instance because Twin Two becomes distressed, the epidural drug can easily be topped off.

With a light dose of drugs in your epidural, you can often deliver both the babies yourself (watching the monitor helps you recognize the start of a contraction). However, there is a higher chance of a forceps or vacuum delivery.

Ultimately, it's your choice, but it is better to have an epidural as a planned procedure than to find you need one during labor, when it might be too late to get one, or to benefit from it much.

Doctor's advice

Pain relief methods

The methods are much the same as for singleton birth, though what's available in your hospital may be different, so talk to your doctor.

Nondrug methods include
- Relaxation
- Massage
- TENS (transcutaneous electrical nerve stimulation)
- Acupuncture
- Birthing pool

Drug methods include
- Nitrous oxide
- Injections, eg fentanyl
- Spinal anesthesia
- Epidural anesthesia
- General anesthetic

Epidural injection Anesthetic is given through a fine tube into the epidural space, and the dose can be topped off if needed.

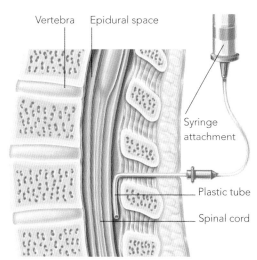

Vertebra   Epidural space

Syringe attachment

Plastic tube

Spinal cord

Vaginal delivery

A vaginal delivery is often possible with twins. It's what most women aim for, but there are risks that you and your health-care professionals need to face.

When can you have a vaginal birth?

If all is well and both twins are head-down, then a vaginal delivery is usually possible, but if the first twin is head down and the second is breech, it's less clear (see p.64). You'll need to discuss the time and method of delivery with your obstetrician between 32 and 36 weeks, but babies' presentations can alter until 36 weeks, so plans may need to change.

Inducing labor

If you haven't gone into labor by 38 weeks, your doctor may suggest inducing you. This is because the placentas can become less effective, putting the babies at risk of growth restriction as a result.

Induction usually starts with a vaginal suppository (or gel) of prostaglandin, a synthetic version of the natural hormones involved in labor. If this doesn't start the process, you may have your water broken (technically called "amniotomy"). After that, you may have an intravenous drip of oxytocin to stimulate contractions.

What happens in a normal delivery?

Once you're in labor, you'll be observed closely. Twin One (the one closest to the cervix) may have a scalp electrode, a tiny sensor that attaches to your baby's head and monitors his or her pulse, while Twin Two is monitored with a belt around your abdomen. The monitor displays your contractions or the pressure inside the uterus, as well as both babies' heartbeats. This is important because a baby's heartbeat can change a lot with each contraction.

The first stage can be very variable and you may at some point want pain relief (see p.66). You can still move around, but it is more difficult to be truly mobile with a twin labor.

Inducing labor If you need the drug oxytocin, you'll be given it via an intravenous drip.

Contractions Your birth partner can be a big help, reassuring you during each contraction.

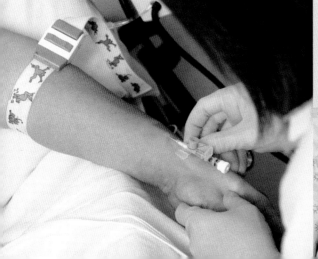

Once your cervix is fully dilated, you need to push with each contraction. You can choose a position that works for you, as long as it doesn't interfere with the monitors. You may stay in the delivery room for the second stage, or be moved to another room or to an operating room. This depends on your hospital's policy and it does not mean surgery is imminent.

It may take an hour or even two for the first baby's head to appear, but after that things usually progress rapidly. Once the first baby is born, you may want to have him on your chest, or your partner can take him. Meanwhile, your doctor checks your belly to confirm the position of the second twin, because this sometimes changes during labor. If Twin Two is breech, the options are to turn the baby around or deliver the baby by the feet or legs. Turning the baby often demands more pain relief.

The second baby is usually born within 30 minutes, but can take longer. If all is well with the baby's heart rate, a delay shouldn't be risky. Once both babies are born, the placentas are delivered with the aid of an injection of oxytocin. This is advisable for twin births, otherwise bleeding can be heavy.

Possible complications

If a twin becomes distressed during the birth, he may open his bowels, so that the amniotic fluid contains visible meconium. The relation of each baby's heart rate to your contractions is very important, too. Heart rate and other readings can indicate how much oxygen your babies are getting. If their oxygen levels are low, you'll probably be given an oxygen mask to boost what reaches your babies, and you may also need urgent help to get that baby out. This could be with the use of a vacuum (suction device) or forceps. Sometimes the distressed baby is out of the reach of instruments like forceps, or your cervix may not be fully dilated yet. In such cases, an emergency cesarean is the answer, so having an epidural in place gives the flexibility of pain relief that you might need.

Anna's birth story

I knew I wanted to try for a vaginal birth and had the support of my husband and doctor. I was induced at 39 weeks. Luckily both babies were head down and doing well. When my contractions grew stronger, I was given an epidural and put on an IV. We were moved into an operating room but I still felt in control and my doctor guided me through when to push. I watched Twin One, my daughter, appear and she was handed to me for a cuddle. Twin Two's position was checked and he was head down, so my water was broken and he was born eight minutes later. Both babies were wrapped and handed to me and our new family was left alone to bond.

Arrival Before long you'll be smiling with your newborn babies in your arms.

Cesarean birth

Over half of all twins are delivered by cesarean section. Although a cesarean birth is a surgical operation, the experience can be a lot more satisfying than many women imagine it will be.

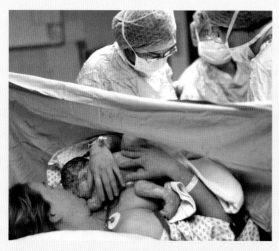

Cesarean birth You should be able to touch or even hold each baby immediately after they are delivered.

Two types of cesarean

A cesarean section (also called C-section) can be planned ahead of time, in which case you'll bypass the process of labor entirely. It can also be performed as an emergency procedure, because one of the babies becomes distressed during labor, for instance, or there's a cord prolapse. In a few rare cases, Twin One is born normally and a cesarean becomes necessary for Twin Two.

A planned (so-called elective) cesarean is common with twins. A lot depends on the position of your babies in the uterus (see pp. 64–65). Other reasons for a cesarean include placenta previa, vasa previa, preeclampsia, and concerns about the growth of one or other twin. Babies who are already stressed don't tolerate labor well, especially since the second

twin has to withstand the contractions that deliver Twin One. These circumstances don't usually arise until the later weeks of pregnancy so it may not be until 35 weeks or so that you know whether you heading for a C-section.

One bonus of knowing in advance that you're having a cesarean is that you'll have also planned what kind of anesthesia you prefer. An epidural for an elective C-section is ideal since you will be awake and won't miss a single precious moment of the birth. Unfortunately, an emergency cesarean can mean general anesthesia if you don't have an epidural in place, though a spinal anesthesia may be possible.

Of course, the other advantage of having an elective C-section is that you can prepare mentally for the procedure. If it's done as an emergency, you may feel bewildered unless you have already accepted the possibility of it happening.

What happens at a cesarean birth

The procedure itself is usually done via a horizontal cut near the bikini line. You'll be lying on your back, tilted slightly to one side to avoid pressure on your major blood vessels. As with most surgeries in and around the pelvis, you will have a catheter to drain urine away, as well as an intravenous drip in your arm. These may stay in for about 12 hours or overnight. And it goes without saying that the procedure won't go ahead until you're properly anesthetized under epidural or general anesthesia. Your partner should be able to be there too, unless you are given general anesthesia.

You'll have a sterile screen in front of you so that you can't see the surgery. Your partner may want to stay behind the screen and hold your hand, or to look in on the surgery site, if the doctors allow it.

Aside from a rummaging or tugging sensation, which most women find odd but not at all unpleasant, there may be a little noise from surgical instruments. Typically this is a bit of clinking and some suction noises. You're unlikely to find it intrusive or troublesome, but it can be surprising unless you know to expect it.

Within minutes, the obstetrician will be lifting your first baby out of your abdomen for you to see. You'll be told as each twin is delivered, and at this point, a doctor can tell you the sex of that baby. The second twin should follow within a minute, and this baby will also be held up for you to see. There's

The once over One of the doctors will check each of your twins soon after they're born.

rarely any delay between twins. Unless the babies need urgent medical attention, your birth partner can take photos or videos, hold the twins, and show them to you. It is sometimes possible for you to have a baby put on your chest right after a cesarean, but it can be difficult to hold them there safely for more than a moment until the procedure is completed.

After the babies are born, the placentas are delivered. The obstetrician checks that your uterus is now empty, then stitches you up in layers. This part of the procedure tends to go by very fast, especially since you have far more exciting things to concentrate on at this stage. You might have stitches or small metal clips in the skin and then a light dressing on top. The whole procedure takes around 30 minutes.

After your cesarean

If all is well, you should be able to leave the operating or delivery room holding your babies. However, your arms may feel weak if you had your epidural topped

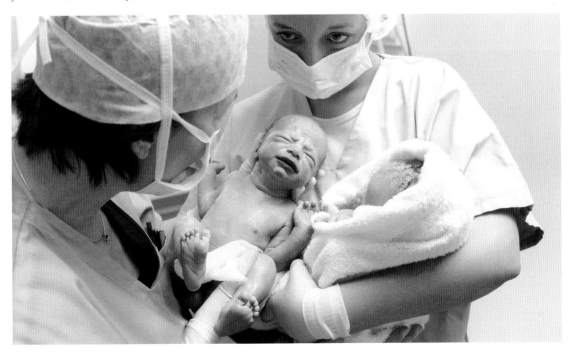

Labor and birth

off for the C-section. And if you had a general anesthesia, cuddling your twins will have to wait until you're fully awake, which may take an hour or more. You can also expect to feel groggy for 24 hours or so if you had a general, so you may not be able to hold your babies securely without help.

Immediately after any cesarean, the nurses will keep a close eye on you to make sure your pulse, temperature, and blood pressure remain stable. They will keep watch on your incision, too, and ask about blood loss. Even with a C-section, the uterus goes through all the normal changes associated with delivery, so you'll have a mixture of blood and fluid discharged from your vagina. This tends to continue for several weeks and you will need to wear pads.

The incision site will feel uncomfortable for a few days if not longer, mostly when you move around or laugh. But it's still a good idea to get moving as soon as you can. Leg movements help reduce the risk of a blood clot (deep vein thrombosis, or DVT). There's no reason why you can't breast-feed after a cesarean, but you may need some help positioning your twins for each feeding. Some moms find that different positions help—for instance, lying on one side avoids having the weight of a baby over the incision. But simply using more cushions on your lap during breast-feeding may also do the trick.

Don't hesitate to ask for help, whether it's for feedings, changing, or just soothing your babies, otherwise it may not be obvious to the staff that you could use an extra pair of hands.

Recovery after the birth is a little slower than with a vaginal delivery. The uterus takes slightly longer to shrink back to its normal size, you may lose a bit more blood, and you can also expect to feel more tired. It is, after all, surgery. Try to make time for pelvic floor exercises (see p.17). These are important after a cesarean too, because the pelvic muscles are always under pressure in late pregnancy. You can usually go home from the hospital in three or four days. Try to take it easy, and concentrate on

Important role Your birth partner can hold and cuddle the babies while you recover from the surgery.

what really matters: your babies and your recovery. If you possibly can, avoid stretching and heavy lifting, but your incision won't pop open when you have a good laugh. It's said that driving a car is better left until six weeks after a C-section, but this isn't always so. Check with your doctor and your insurer.

Emotions

You can expect to go through any or all the emotions a new twin mom experiences. After a cesarean, many women feel overwhelming relief that their babies are safely here. In fact, most moms who deliver by cesarean are very satisfied, and many say they would choose a cesarean again in future.

Others are more ambivalent about the procedure, and may feel disappointed or even cheated especially if they had their hearts set on a normal delivery. They sometimes feel that in some way it wasn't a "real birth." It is of course a real birth, and these babies are very much yours no matter how they arrived on the day itself. It's not the delivery that makes a family. It is all the other times together in the coming years. However, if you do have negative feelings about the birth, it can be useful to talk them through with your doctor and with other moms of twins.

Once a C-section, not always a C-section

You may want to have another baby sometime in the future. If you had a C-section this time it doesn't necessarily mean that you will need one next time. It depends on why you had one for your twins. If it was for breech babies, for instance, that reason may not recur. Placenta previa, cord prolapse, and fetal distress are also conditions that don't always strike twice. On the other hand, if you have a narrow pelvis, that's for life. Chances are that after a cesarean for twins you can have a vaginal delivery, or at least go into labor and see what happens. When the time comes, you and your obstetrician can discuss the option of VBAC (vaginal birth after cesarean).

Katy's birth story

I was initially disappointed when advised to consider a cesarean, but I wouldn't change anything about the day my twins were born. There was a fantastic atmosphere in the room, the team were really relaxed and supportive.

It was reassuring to know that experts were close if they were needed, but luckily both boys were fine. Twin One was cleaned, wrapped, and handed to me, and then on to Dad once Twin Two was ready to meet me.

During the procedure I didn't want the screen lowered since I'm a bit squeamish, but it is amazing to see the photos and I'm grateful to the anesthesiologist who took them. I worried about the recovery, but by day three I could walk around with ease. My scar is small and has now faded to a neat line.

Back home Once you return home you can take time to enjoy getting to know your new family.

Your babies' arrival

Your new babies

Congratulations! You did it! The months of planning and panicking and wondering and waiting are over: you three have made it across the start line. Welcome to the club.

Squished and sleepy

Your tiny twins will look a bit squished for the first few days until they uncurl; this is hardly surprising given how snug they have been in the weeks leading up to the birth.

Your babies will probably sleep a lot initially, giving you time to study them in detail and marvel at the fact that you grew two people in your belly.

Knowing who is who

If you have identical twins, consider dressing them in different clothes. It may seem silly, but until personality traits, characteristics, and differences in movement become apparent, it will ensure that you do not get mixed up! Painting a nail with nail polish is another way to be sure who's who.

Early days

Your newborn babies have very little head control, so you need to make sure they are well supported. Newborns startle easily at loud noises and their arms may fly out to their sides. If your babies get upset and cry, they will not shed tears; that happens in a few months.

Your babies may look pink because of the higher red blood count in their bodies, but immature circulation may leave their hands and feet cold. Babies cannot easily control their temperature and can overheat, so the number of blankets required depends on the ambient temperature.

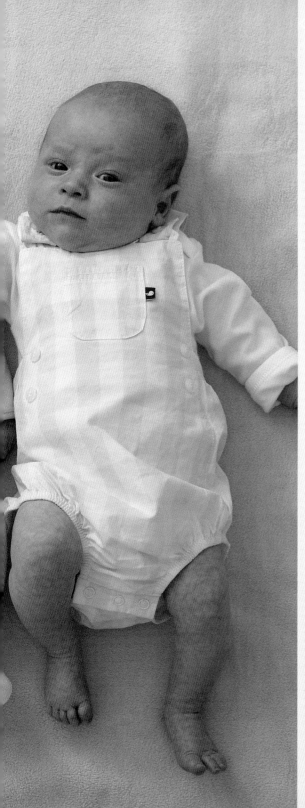

Your babies may still have some "vernix" in the creases of their ears, arms, and groin. This waxy coating protects their skin in the uterus and will come off after their first few baths.

Babies often have skin imperfections, tiny white spots, or little rashes that gradually disappear. Flat pink or red spots at the base of babies' necks or over eyelids are commonly referred to as stork bites. They may be more noticeable when your babies cry, but will fade over time.

Head shape

The shape of your babies' heads will depend, to an extent, on the birth; cesarean babies will have rounder heads than those born vaginally. Laying your babies on their backs to sleep may accentuate uneven head shapes, but this is necessary to prevent sudden infant death syndrome (SIDS). Once they gain head control their head shapes will even out.

Your babies have two soft spots on the top of their head called the fontanelles, which are spaces between the growing skull bones. These fuse as your babies grow. You may see the fontanelle at the front of your babies' scalps—it will feel squishy but is protected by a tough inner skin. Never press on the fontanelle. You may see it pulsating from time to time, but this is normal. If you notice that your babies' fontanelles have sunk, contact your doctor since it could be a sign of serious dehydration.

Umbilical cord

Your twins will each have an umbilical stump where their cords were cut. You will need to keep these areas clean and dry to prevent infection. When the stumps fall off, after a week or two, you will see your babies' belly buttons.

Spot the difference Besides making it easier to tell them apart, dressing twins in different clothes also helps them develop their own individual identity.

Bonding

Bonding with twins may be different than bonding with one baby, but rest assured there is more than enough love to go around.

Bonding with two babies

As a multiple mom you are likely to have mixed emotions when you hear experts and singleton moms talk about the importance of bonding in the first few minutes, hours, and days. It is unrealistic to assume that you can bond with twins in the same way as you can with a singleton because you will have less time with each baby.

You may not be able to lose yourself in eye contact with just one baby, or snuggle up in such a way that both babies are nestled next to your heart, but remember that your twin babies have each other, as well as you, and there are plenty of things that you can do to ensure you create special life-long bonds with both babies.

It is perfectly fine to feel overwhelmed initially, but just by being with your babies, being attentive, caring, and making sure that they are fed, clean, and cared for will ensure you bond with them in the process of getting through each day.

Bonding tools

Try to have some one-on-one time with each twin. Rather than setting aside specific time each day to "bond," which is likely to be an unrealistic goal, see each baby "chore" as an opportunity for individual

Baby bonding Little interactions, such as eye contact, holding hands, and babbling conversations, act as building blocks for your relationship with each baby.

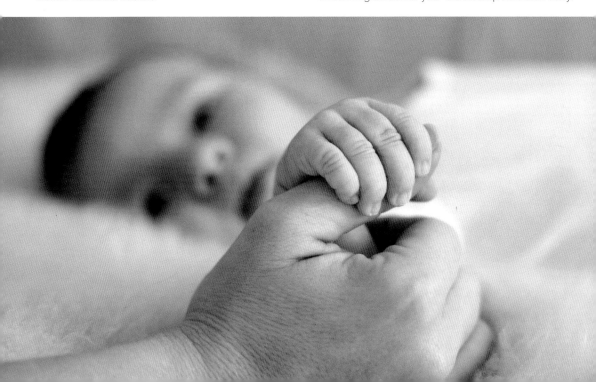

attention. Even the most advanced twin mom can only change one diaper at a time, so perhaps incorporate some massage, cuddling, eye contact, and smiles into the task—who knows, you may even start looking forward to diaper o'clock!

In addition to physical closeness and eye contact, you can use your voice to bond with your babies. Talk and sing to your little ones; your voice will be familiar to them from their time in the uterus and they will be calmed and reassured by it. The advantage of using your voice as a tool to aid bonding is that you can soothe and build relationships with both babies, even when you are unable to hold them both at the same time.

Belated bonding

Your birth experience can affect the bonding process. Complications may have meant that doctors could not follow your birth plan, or perhaps your babies had to spend some time in the neonatal intensive care unit (NICU) (see pp.88-89), but remember that you have a lifetime to create magic memories and strong bonds with your babies. Try to relax and make time to enjoy them, safe in the knowledge that this is the best thing you can do for your relationship with them, as well as for their long-term development.

There will be days when one baby demands more of your time and you may worry that you are not bonding as well with the less-demanding baby. Or the opposite may be true: you may feel so exhausted by the demands of the fussier baby that you feel a stronger bond with the more easy-going sibling. This will switch and change and even itself out over time. Treating your babies fairly does not necessarily mean treating them equally at all times.

Your partner is in a unique and fortunate position. Twin partners often report that they had a more active role in their babies' lives from an earlier stage—when mom is busy with one baby, there is one for them to cuddle, too!

Long-term feelings

Ask the parents

Many moms feel a little disappointed if they can't spend time with their babies immediately after the birth. A few even consider themselves a little inadequate if they don't feel a sudden rush of love for their twins.

But there's no need to worry. Those early moments and feelings, as lovely and precious as they often are, don't dictate how you will relate to your twins as they grow up. A baby does not instantly have feelings for the first person who touched them. Research shows that a baby's attachments develop over a period of many months. A deep, enduring relationship depends on being fed, cuddled, and nurtured in every sense.

One-on-one time Spending time with each baby separately not only allows you to bond, but also helps you notice the little differences between them.

Feeding twins

There are two babies and two breasts, but it doesn't always add up to easy. It is possible to breast-feed twins, but there are other options that may work better for you and your babies.

Breast-feeding

The best place to learn is in the hospital. The staff will help you latch your babies on, teach you how to check that they are in the correct position, and show you how to make yourself as comfortable as possible. Milk is created on a supply and demand basis, but it can take a few days for your milk to "come in."

Premature babies may need to be tube fed but can still benefit from breast milk. If your milk is yet to come in ask if the hospital has a milk bank. Some women donate breast milk and it is possible that your babies could benefit from their generosity until you are ready to feed them yourself.

You can feed your babies together or separately. Feeding them together takes practice and perseverance, but it saves time and puts both babies on the same schedule. You might prefer to nurse your babies separately by staggering the feedings and nursing them one at a time. A staggered approach to feeding takes longer, but allows you to have one-on-one time with each baby and get the hang of breast-feeding.

Once your milk is in, you might consider using breast pads. These are soft, absorbent disks worn inside your bra to absorb leakage.

Tandem feeding

The football hold is the most popular way to nurse twins simultaneously. For the first few days, the three of you will need help positioning cushions and latching on, but as you all gain experience and confidence, this can be a very time-efficient way to feed them.

Football hold Tandem feeding takes practice, but can help establish a routine that will give you some precious baby-free minutes during the day.

Hold one baby under each arm and guide their mouths to your nipples. You may want to assign each baby their own breast, or change at each feeding. If one baby is much smaller than the other, consider swapping breasts at each feeding, at least initially, to stimulate them both and encourage supply. Breast-feeding takes practice, so try to stay relaxed and take things one feeding at a time.

If one baby is hungrier than the other and they always nurse at the same breast, you may become lop-sided at times but this usually settles down and it is unlikely anyone else will notice.

The eye contact between all three of you when you tandem nurse is a powerful reminder of the physical bond that you share and a unique twin mom experience.

Little and often

Initially your babies will need feeding little and often—on average every three hours. As their tummies grow, they will be able to manage more food and will need feeding less frequently. You can nurse on demand, but keep in mind that it is highly unlikely both babies will "demand" to be fed simultaneously, so you may find you are constantly nursing a baby if you try this approach. If your babies are very premature, you may be advised to wake them regularly to be fed, otherwise they may choose sleeping over eating… and you need them to grow bigger and stronger.

Express yourself!

Ask a breast-feeding adviser at the hospital to show you how to express your milk to encourage it to come in. You can express with a handheld or electric pump. You can rent or buy breast pumps if you would like to continue breast-feeding when you leave the hospital.

Expressing milk means that you can build a milk supply and indulge in the occasional guilt-free snooze, safe in the knowledge that your babies are benefiting from being fed breast milk while you benefit from some much-needed sleep. Expressed breast milk can be stored for up to three months in the freezer. Frozen milk should be defrosted in the fridge. Breast milk can be stored in the fridge ideally for no more than 24 hours, though it is likely to be safe for as long as five days if your fridge is below 39°F (4°C).

Ask the parents

Benefits of breast-feeding twins

Breast-feeding isn't for everyone, and breast-feeding twins is demanding, but there are certain benefits which mean you might want to give it a try it and see how you do.

- It's free.
- It passes on some of your immunity.
- It is available on demand and at the right temperature.
- It is easier to digest than formula so your babies are less likely to suffer from constipation.
- It helps you regain your pre-pregnancy shape more quickly.
- There are no bottles to sterilize.
- It may protect you from some cancers later in life.

Breast is best Breast-feeding will help protect your twins from infections and illnesses in their first year.

Breasts, balloons, knots, and nipples...

Your breasts may become very full and hard (engorged), so expressing some milk before nursing will help you feel more comfortable. It will also make it easier for your babies to latch on. Imagine your breast is a balloon and the nipple is the knot: if the balloon is too full it is difficult to get to the knot. Your babies may experience the same frustrations trying to get to your nipple if your breasts are too full. By expressing a little, your babies can latch on more easily. You can also save the precious expressed milk and put it toward a complete feeding another time.

Caffeine and breast-feeding

A small amount of everything you eat and drink will be passed on to your babies, but the good news for sleep-deprived twin moms is that you can reach for a caffeinated pickup. If you limit yourself to two to three cups a day, the level of caffeine passed on via your breast milk will be negligible. Some moms report that their babies are harder to settle down if they have had a lot of coffee, and if you notice a correlation between your caffeine intake and sleepless nights it is worthwhile to reduce your consumption or switching to decaffeinated coffee to see if things improve.

Alcohol and breast-feeding

The guidelines for drinking alcohol in pregnancy ease up in breast-feeding; limit your intake to one or two drinks once or twice a week. Your weight and whether you drink alcohol with food or on an empty stomach will determine how long it takes the alcohol to enter your breast milk. You will need to allow a

Expressing milk Place the pump firmly over your nipple to form an airtight seal and pump rhythmically until you have expressed the required amount of milk.

Storing safe Before you store the expressed milk in the fridge for future use, be sure to label the bottles with the date and the time at which the milk was expressed.

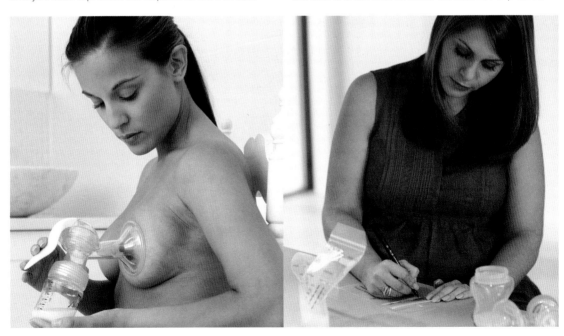

couple of hours for your body to be completely clear of one drink of alcohol.

If you would like to enjoy an alcoholic drink at a time least likely to affect your babies, it is best to nurse your babies first, and then have a drink. When your babies next need feeding, the alcohol level in your breast milk will be minimal. Newborns will need feeding more often, so it is best to avoid alcohol until they are older.

Mastitis

Mastitis is a condition that causes your breasts to become inflamed. Your breasts may become red, hard, swollen, hot, or sore, and you may even develop a fever or flulike symptoms. You may feel a lump in your breast caused by milk getting into the breast tissue rather than the milk ducts.

If you suspect you have mastitis don't stop nursing since this will make things worse. See your doctor as soon as possible, she may prescribe antibiotics if you have developed an infection.

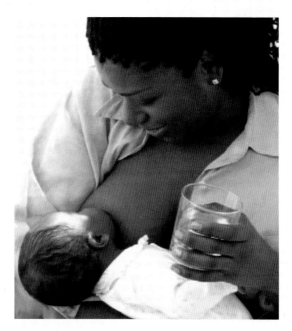

Stay hydrated Breast-feeding can dehydrate you, so remember to drink water throughout the day, and try to drink a glass of water every time you breast-feed.

Ask the parents

Help yourself to help your babies

It can take a while to get used to breast-feeding one baby, let alone two, so try not to put too much pressure on yourself. The following tips may help you to get started.

• Get comfortable, use a V-shaped feeding cushion or pillows so you feel supported.

• Don't be shy. Breast-feeding twins is not discreet, but it is wonderful. If you feel a bit uncomfortable breast-feeding in public, know that with time, you'll become more confident.

• Stay hydrated, it's thirsty work! Your urine should be pale colored, which will confirm that you are drinking enough.

• Breast-feeding usually gives you a big appetite. Try to choose nutritious foods.

• Tandem nursing takes practice but can help establish a routine that is more likely to give you some baby-free minutes during the day.

• Go to a breast-feeding group for support.

• Use a breast pump to express milk, and also to encourage supply.

• Be flexible: mixed nursing with some formula can give you a break.

Vitamin D is passed on to your babies through your milk and helps bones and teeth to grow healthily. However, exclusively breast-fed babies should receive a daily vitamin D supplement of 400 IU as your milk will not supply enough for their needs.

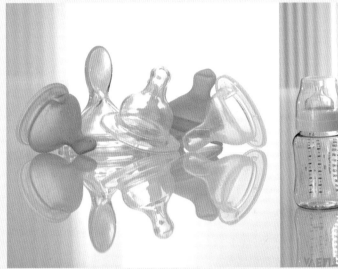

Nipples The nipples should ideally be shaped to fit your babies' mouths. You may need to try out a few to find which nipples suits your babies best.

Bottles As with most baby products, bottles come in a variety of styles. Choose one that is unbreakable and has a wide neck since they're easier to fill and clean.

Bottle and combination feeding

Breast-feeding twins is not for everyone and modern formula provides a nutritious alternative that can help keep mom happy and babies healthy.

Make sure preparation areas and surfaces are clean and follow the manufacturer's instructions so that you use the correct ratio of powder and water. If you use a scoop to measure the formula, use a sterilized knife to level the powder before you put the desired quantity into the bottle and add the water.

Make up feedings as you need them, using cooled boiled water—not softened or mineral water since this could alter the composition of the formula. Always follow the manufacturer's instructions and be sure to check the temperature of the formula: it should feel just warm against your wrist.

Prepared formula is more expensive than powder, but comes with the reassurance that it is perfectly balanced and can be served warm or at room temperature. Consider using prepared formula when you are traveling, or at night to maximize your sleep window.

Your newborn babies will initially have about eight feedings in 24 hours. The disadvantage of formula feeding is all the bottle preparation and sterilizing involved. However, it allows you to see how much your babies are consuming and means your partner can become involved in the process, too.

There is a wide range of bottles and nipples available for use with formula or expressed breast milk, and you might want to try a couple of styles to see which your babies prefer. Initially, you will want a slow-flow nipple that limits the speed at which milk flows into your babies' mouths; as they get bigger and more competent at feeding, you can change to a faster-flow nipple.

If you would like to combine breast- and bottle-feeding you might want to choose a nipple that more closely resembles the shape of your nipple since this will help your babies to go from breast to bottle.

When bottle-feeding, cradle your baby in the crook of your arm in a semi-upright position, ensuring the head is well supported. Hold the bottle so that the formula or expressed breast milk fills the nipple: this will reduce the amount of air your baby swallows, which can cause discomfort.

You can hold and bottle-feed both babies together but it requires practice. Alternatively, place one baby in a bouncy chair and feed with one hand while you hold and feed the other baby. Swap babies to ensure both get some cuddling.

Keeping track

The 24/7 demands of two young babies can leave you sleep deprived and unable to rely on your tired mind to accurately recall the precise details of who fed when and how much. To make things a bit easier for yourself, consider buying a notebook and keeping a log of feeding patterns.

By dividing the pages into columns you can jot down feeding times and quantities. Three columns headed Twin/ Time/ Quantity would allow you to keep track of feedings. This can be particularly useful if you are breast- and bottle-feeding when you may lose track of which twin was breast-fed last and who had a bottle.

Devise a system that works for you and change the headings and information logged accordingly, for example if you are breast-feeding exclusively it may be worthwhile to note the duration of time each twin spends at each breast.

Needless to say, as the three of you establish a routine and gain confidence in the familiarity of your daily pattern the notebook will become redundant but for those first few weeks it may prove reassuring.

Divide and drool If each partner feeds one baby, it is less time consuming and an opportunity for one-on-one bonding; switch babies for the next feeding.

Practical help

To make the initial period after birth as easy as possible it is important that you have the practical and emotional support you need.

Friends and family

Family and friends will be lining up to come and see your new arrivals, and will often be more than happy to help out. Maximize the help offered by articulating what you would like people to do: cook a meal, do the dishes, or give the twins a feeding so you can rest. Make sure everyone who visits does something useful, otherwise you will find yourself making coffee for well-wishers who leave you even more exhausted.

Be nice to relatives! You will need their help, but it is important that you feel able to express how and when you would like things done. If you have older children, perhaps a friend could take the twins for a walk so you can spend some time with them, or perhaps the older children would prefer to be taken out for a non-twin adventure.

When your friends and family give you a few precious minutes to yourself, try to relax. Resist the temptation to clean the house, and enjoy some calm, quiet time instead. Put your feet up and read a magazine, call a friend, or venture out for a baby-free coffee. A change of scenery and some fresh air can be invigorating, but you might be surprised that despite being desperate for a break, you want to get back to your babies the minute you said goodbye.

Helpful visitors Grandparents, family, and friends will flock to see your twins and are often happy to help out.

Professional help

In addition to family and friends, you might want to consider enlisting professional help for the first few weeks. Your bank balance will determine what kind of help you have and for how long, but there are also other factors to consider such as what type of person will fit into your household.

Baby nurse On duty 24 hours a day, six days a week, and helps with all aspects of newborn care. They usually sleep with the babies and, if breast-fed, will take the babies to mom when it is time to nurse.

Night nurse Typically works 8pm–8am. They not only allow you to have uninterrupted sleep, but also help guide your babies into a sleep routine, too.

Nanny Can live in or out, but typically works at least 40 hours a week and can provide a reassuring and experienced pair of hands to help share the tasks. The babies are their primary focus, although many are prepared to help with baby-related chores around the house, too. This will need to be agreed at the interview.

Au pair Not technically an employee, but more a "member of the family" so make sure she will fit in and benefit your rapidly expanding household. Au pairs expect to have their own room, and traditionally work five hours a day on light housework and child care, but don't usually have sole charge.

Doula Provide practical and emotional support during pregnancy, childbirth, and early parenthood.

Mother's helper Helps with all aspects of child care, meal preparation, errands, and light housework. The job is varied and a parent or caregiver is usually in the home as well.

A helpful hand Getting someone to help you with your daily household chores will give you more time to take care of, and bond with, your little ones.

House cleaner Not an obvious child-care suggestion, but if delegating the vacuuming and dusting to someone else helps keep you calm, then it is money well spent. It means you can enjoy the rare moments of twin cuddling time without having to put up with the nagging guilt of undone housework.

Choose carefully

You need to feel comfortable around the stranger who is set to become an integral member of Team Twin, so consider a "coffee cup interview" and if you struggle to feel relaxed with them while enjoying a coffee and a bit of chitchat, it is unlikely that you will feel comfortable with them after the birth.

Determining the kind of help you would like will help you to identify what sort of professional would be best for you and your family. Contact local twins groups and ask other parents what kind of help they had, where they found it, and what their experiences were. You may find that they highlight pros and cons with the benefit of hindsight that you can learn from.

Special Care and Neonatal Intensive Care

In over 40 percent of twin births, one or both babies will spend time in special care or the neonatal intensive care unit (NICU). It's good to know about them.

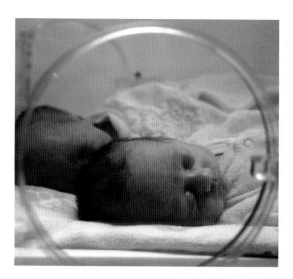

Incubator These keep babies warm and protected from infection. The portholes allow access to your babies.

What premature babies need

Babies born pre-term have missed out on those last vital days in the uterus—the best incubator of all. Some will need to be in special care nurseries and others that need more help will go to the neonatal intensive care unit (NICU). In both units your baby will get needed warmth and regular nourishment, help with feeding, and protection from infection.

What Special Care can do

Special care nurseries, also called Level 2 nurseries, take care of moderately ill babies, born at more than 32 weeks. The incubator will keep your babies warm and they may be fed through a tube if they can't yet suck: this can be formula, but it's even better if it's your breast milk since it contains valuable immune cells and antibodies. These nurseries are often places where babies who are medically stable are kept until they gain enough weight to go home. They may have minor problems such as jaundice requiring phototherapy, inability to maintain their body temperature outside the incubator, or minor infections but they are generally not severely ill.

What NICU is like

The NICU offers a high staff-to-baby ratio. Babies in the NICU are surrounded by a lot of high-tech machinery. Your tiny twins may have one or more intravenous drips and other lines, as well as all the equipment that goes into delivering fluids and monitoring vital signs. Their breathing, heart rate, and blood pressure will be monitored constantly. Pressure is often measured through a tiny arterial line that goes straight into a blood vessel. From time to time, there'll be tests such as X-rays and scans to assess progress and preempt any possible complications. Scans are especially important for monitoring how a baby's brain is doing. Alarms sound regularly, for other babies if not for yours. Many babies in NICU are on ventilators. In the NICU, you can rest assured that your babies are getting the best possible care, but all in all it's a busy, noisy place, which can bewilder parents.

What you can do

While NICU can do a huge amount for your babies, with the long-term outcomes improving all the time, there's one thing that only you can provide. Premature babies need your love just as much as they need the most advanced medical care. Even when babies are in an incubator, you can show them your love. Ask the staff how to help with daily care, such as diaper changes and feedings, and hold your baby during any procedures that may be necessary. Your touch is calming and reassuring, and plays an important role in bonding, too. Skin-to-skin care (also called kangaroo care) is especially beneficial since it helps regulate a baby's breathing and boosts development. If both twins are in the NICU, you may be able to do this with your partner, or else hold one baby at a time. Don't forget you can also take pictures, videos, and footprints of your twins. These make precious keepsakes, but check with the staff first.

Feeding

If possible, express breast milk. This is particularly good for pre-term babies, and the process of expressing gives you something special to do for your twins and may calm you, too. There should be a pump available for your use, so ask.

Emotions

It's natural to feel worried, confused, panicky, sad, reassured, happy, or ecstatic—sometimes all in one day. And you may feel different emotions for each baby, depending on what is happening.

Parents of babies in the NICU rightly describe it as a roller-coaster experience. You'll meet other parents there who may share their stories with you, but don't assume the same things are happening to your babies as theirs. When you have questions, always ask the staff members who are used to dealing with concerns. There is also a counselor attached to these units.

Occasionally, doctors will suggest a different hospital for each baby. This may be medically necessary, but should never happen for the hospital's convenience. Before agreeing to any transfers, find out as much information as you can by talking to the doctors and nurses on staff.

Close contact Spending time with your babies reassures them and has benefits for all of you.

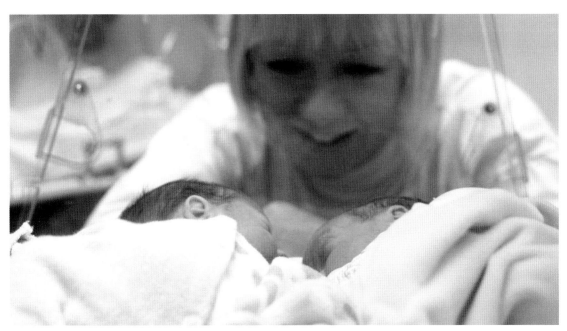

How you might be feeling

When you were pregnant, it might have been impossible for you to imagine what life would be like post birth, so go easy on yourself if you do not instantly feel at ease with your babies.

Getting to know the new you

In addition to learning about your new babies, it may take time for you to get to know the new you—the woman newly promoted to Twin Mom. Like any new job it can take a while to settle in.

Becoming a mom is life changing, and becoming a multiple mom in an instant can be overwhelming. Don't be hard on yourself and don't put pressure on yourself for everything to be perfect. Love your babies and be certain that bit by bit, day by day, you will continue to learn more about each other.

Having twins is exciting and rewarding, but also very demanding. Try to have a little time for yourself each day, even if it is just 20 minutes to take an uninterrupted bath. Ask family or friends to watch the babies for you while you shut yourself away, and shut your eyes and recharge.

Feeling tired comes with the twin territory, and fatigue, combined with the intensity of your new life, can prompt negative feelings from time to time. Try not to feel guilty for having these feelings. It is normal to wonder, in exhausted moments, if you are up to the job. You are. These feelings won't last and you will soon get the hang of life with twins.

Change and change again

Babies change and grow rapidly, which is a mixed blessing. Just when you have got the hang of putting on onesies and little hats, it is time to get the hang of putting four little shoes on four little feet, and just when you think diaper changes are a breeze, your increasingly independent little ones decide they no longer want to lie down while you change them!

The first three months can be a sleepless blur, but suddenly you are not where you were. Know that whatever you are struggling with is just a phase, and enjoy the precious moments that you treasure at each stage of development, because these too will change.

Being a twin mom will teach you many things, challenge you in many ways, and teach you a love you didn't think possible. You will experience highs, lows, and loss of sleep, and although you may not love every single minute, I guarantee you wouldn't have it any other way.

Pamper yourself Though your babies will have most of your attention, take some time out to sit back and relax, so you don't burn out.

Postpartum depression

When you've just had a baby, it is normal to feel tired, confused, and even bewildered. Even if you're not a first-time parent you may feel a little out of your depth with two new babies. At times you may be tearful or sleepless, or perhaps you find it hard to concentrate or are unable to summon up any interest in sex.

It's only to be expected when you have two demanding little people to care for. But sometimes these feelings are more severe or long-lasting. Sleeplessness can be very draining because you can't sleep even though you are tired. Instead you lie awake worrying. You may also wake at night although your babies are sound asleep. Some women with depression wake extremely early, long before their babies need feeding. You may also have appetite changes, mood swings, and an inability to enjoy much at all, whether it's the babies or a favorite TV program. Those symptoms suggest a slide from new-parent exhaustion into postpartum depression (PPD).

PPD often starts a couple of weeks after the birth, but sometimes it doesn't appear until months afterward. On the other hand, some women develop symptoms in pregnancy, and these continue or worsen after their babies arrive. Often there are anxiety symptoms, too, such as a pounding heart or racing pulse, sweating or shortness of breath.

PPD is amazingly common. Some 10–15 percent of new moms get it, and so do some dads. This suggests it has very little to do with hormones. It is also a bit more common when you have twins. There's nothing inherently depressing about twins, it's just that fatigue and stress are probably factors. The important thing is to get help if you have any feelings that may be above and beyond those any new parent has. Speak to someone you trust, whether it's your doctor or a close friend. Owning up to feelings of PPD is not a weakness; it's a sign that you recognize the need to be at your best.

PPD Emotional support and practical advice can help a new twin mom to overcome postpartum depression.

By and large, women with PPD don't have thoughts of harming themselves or their babies, but when they do it's vital to get help urgently. There are also a few women who develop more unusual symptoms, such as hearing voices or having delusions. If this happens, you should also seek help immediately (see below).

Treating PPD can involve just talking to someone, or having more formal counseling. Sometimes antidepressants help, and contrary to popular opinion they're not habit forming. Even if you're breast-feeding, it's usually possible to find one that is suitable. The main thing is to acknowledge how you feel and take that first step to recovery for your sake and that of your family. Rest assured that even with the most severe types of postpartum illness, your babies are most unlikely to be taken away from you.

The year ahead

Your babies' development

There's nothing quite as fascinating as watching your twins grow and develop. Reaching milestones is exciting, but don't expect your babies to reach each of these at exactly the same time.

Size and weight

Most twins aren't exactly the same size. One of them may weigh more right from birth, or your babies may have heads of a slightly different shape, even if they both arrived by cesarean section. Size discrepancies usually even out in time. However, boys are often a bit larger and heavier than girls. Over the years, identical twins grow to be more alike in size, while so-called fraternal twins tend to become more different in their physical growth.

Twins are usually lighter and smaller than singleton babies born at the same stage of pregnancy. If your babies were pre-term, they're likely to be even lighter. But your twins will grow fast, and as a rough guide, by the second birthday there are hardly any differences between a premature baby and one born on time.

Sizing up Your twins may not be the same size and weight at birth but in time the difference can become less obvious.

Making the most of movement

Babies develop from the head down. Neck and arms grow in size and strength before the lower body. When your babies first sit up, the legs are little more than stabilizers to take body weight. But soon trunk and hip muscles grow stronger, and before long your twins will be on the move. Most babies crawl, but before this they often go through a stage of commando-creeping on their bellies.

You can help your twins develop neck and back control by letting each of them play on their front at some point every day. But they should still sleep on their backs at night and during any naps (see p.109). Once they're on the move, whether it's crawling, commando-creeping, or even rolling, they're more

likely to get into trouble. Accidents around the home are fairly common with twins. Keep a close eye on your babies and make sure their environment is safe. That's not as simple as it sounds, as you have to keep one step ahead of their development. The other challenge is to make your home safe without making it boring. A padded cell would no doubt be safe, but it wouldn't stimulate the senses or help development.

How babies learn

As a baby grows, the brain makes connections between nerve cells. Whatever a baby hears, sees, tastes, smells, or touches forges new links from one cell to another. Repeating each experience reinforces that particular connection. As your twins develop, increasingly complex connections build up in their brains, and that is what makes each person unique—even those who started off with exactly the same genes as someone else.

Your babies have an inborn timetable for development. They are likely to sit up and hold a cup from around six months, crawl at around eight months, and make recognizable words from nine months. Within that broad schedule there's a lot of individual variation, though the sequence of development is constant—sitting comes before standing, for instance. As a parent you can stimulate your babies every step of the way and help them make the most of each opportunity. That's not the same as pushing your babies: it's about giving them chances to build on their full potential.

Not the same

It's really important for your babies' development that you treat your twins as individuals. This will benefit them in terms of both their learning and their behavior. And they truly are individuals. Some babies develop faster than others. Of course, it may seem obvious that fraternal twins are no more alike than any other siblings, but identical twins don't always reach the commonly recognized milestones at the same time either, so don't be too surprised if one of your babies walks or says his first word a week or two earlier than his twin. The other one will surely follow in his own time.

Parents can be very competitive about their babies' growth and abilities. But putting on weight or passing major milestones such as crawling or talking aren't measures of intelligence. Try to avoid labeling your twins because if you find yourself thinking of one as "the fast one," the other baby will almost inevitably be cast as "the slow one." Each baby develops in his own unique way and the timing is far less critical than most moms imagine. But always check with your pediatrician if you are seriously concerned.

Acquiring skills Your twins will each develop at their own pace. It's natural for your babies to follow slightly different schedules.

Learning language

For the first eight weeks of life, babies make noises such as crying and straining. From then on, they add laughing, chuckling, and cooing to their repertoire—all delightful sounds, especially when your babies respond to each other. Between six months and a year is the stage of "vocal play," when babies enjoy making a huge variety of sounds. They often babble to each other as well as to you, but they also babble alone.

A baby's first word is actually a culmination of months of preparation. By the time your twins say something recognizable at around a year, they will already know a lot about the world. Intellect and understanding always outstrip ability to speak, and let's face it, your babies have been busy taking in information since before they were born.

Language skills are honed by imitating others, and this is the challenge when you have twins. Sometimes (but not always) twins can be a little slower at perfecting their language skills. Immature speech can persist longer, what they say may be simpler or shorter, and vocabulary is sometimes smaller, too. Perhaps that's no real surprise since it's hard to give each one stimulation. Often you could be busy with one baby while briefly talking to the other one. Or you'll address both of them together. It's really important to talk to each baby separately as much as you can. Make eye contact so that each baby knows who you're speaking to. And use each twin's name, too, ideally at the start of the sentence. Babies respond to their names from the age of five months, if not before. But to get that response going, you need to start using names much earlier than that.

It's lovely to look at books with a twin tucked under each arm. You don't have to stop doing this, but try also to read stories separately to your babies when possible. The best thing you can do is to give each twin individual time and attention. It will be a challenge because life is busy, but routine chores such as diaper-changing are opportunities, too. One-on-one time with each twin is a great way to stimulate language skills, and it's rewarding for you also.

Baby talk Spend one-on-one time with each of your twins. Talking, singing rhymes, and eye contact all help them each develop language skills.

Together time Twins can have fun interacting and babbling to each other and sharing toys when they're sitting close together.

Boosting concentration

Looking at it from a twin's point of view, it's great having company all the time, but it can also be a little distracting. When one of your babies decides to use a shape-sorter, play with saucepans, or study a bunch of keys closely, there's someone else who wants to muscle in on the fun. That can make it hard to explore the world fully. It may also be an obstacle to your twins learning how to concentrate and stay on task, which is an important life skill in so many areas.

Of course, there's no need to separate your babies all the time; that would be difficult as well as unkind. But when one twin wants to do their own thing, you can sometimes help by engaging the other twin with something else. If you have someone else around, perhaps your partner or a willing grandparent, you could also consider separate outings and activities from time to time. These need not be elaborate or expensive. It might just be a trip to the park in a borrowed single stroller, or some time sitting on the floor with a tray puzzle. Twins undoubtedly learn a lot from each other, but it's also nice for each baby to have a little space of their own sometimes. This can help their social and even physical development.

You can also help your twins learn to concentrate by minimizing interruptions. While a routine may be desirable—and even essential, especially if you have to go out to work—there's little to gain by organizing your twins' lives so rigidly that they get too little time to play.

Babies like to experiment with things, to bang things together and make noise, to drop toys to see if they bounce, and to build towers out of unlikely objects. They need unstructured play like this. If you interrupt play frequently so that they rarely get this type of free-range playtime, they may have trouble developing the skills that help them concentrate and learn.

Time out Your twins enjoy each other's company, but also need their individual space to learn to concentrate.

Your twins will no doubt make a lot of noise with their playthings, adding to this with shrieks of delight, and the occasional howls of protest when they are squabbling over a toy. These sounds are inevitable and usually healthy. But excess background noise hinders mental skills, so try not to leave the television on when nobody is watching, or have the radio on all the time.

Your babies always have each other, but they can have other friends, too. It's good for them to meet other babies, both twins and singletons. Your twins are unlikely to make real playmates at this age however, because it's usually not until around three years old that children really play with others. But it is still beneficial for them to get to know other children. Going to parent and baby groups regularly is one way of doing this.

97

Relationships with your babies and partner

Your twins will affect every relationship you have. Their arrival signals the start of an adventure, a journey to be shared and treasured—and sometimes, just endured—with your partner and other family members.

Your babies

Watching two distinct personalities emerge simultaneously is one of the many perks of being a parent of twins. Twins share a unique bond and will experience the world as a team as well as individuals.

Your babies will be comforted by each other's familiar presence, but will soon be vying for your attention. Ensure you make both babies feel loved, wanted, and valued as individuals.

As your twins grow, you may expect them to be each other's playmate, but don't be disappointed if they occasionally seem unaware of each other. Twins, like singleton babies, engage in "parallel play" and will sit side by side occupied with their own toy.

This is an important developmental phase in which children slowly begin to understand their sense of self. As they grow, their interest in each other and level of interaction will grow and, around three, will move from parallel to cooperative play.

Twins are often better at sharing than their singleton peers, but they can be just as prone to jealousy and possessiveness. Calm, consistent, and fair guidelines will be necessary to overcome the challenges that arise with these tendencies.

Parallel play To avoid conflict, give your twins separate toys to play with when they want to play alone and not with each other.

Parents and partners It's great playing parents together, but also spend time alone with your partner to avoid misunderstandings and resentment.

You and your babies

Treat your twins fairly, not equally. There will be hours and days when one needs your attention more than the other, but this will balance itself out.

Accept that sometimes you can only deal with one baby at a time. Make sure that the baby you are not tending to is safe and remind yourself that you are doing the best you can, which is good enough.

You may not be able to bond with twins in the same way that you can with one baby, but the three of you share an incredible history and connection that is the basis of a very strong and special bond (see p.78).

You may worry about how to nurture two babies to ensure that they have a strong sense of self, as well as enjoying the novelty that they came as a pair. Remember that your babies may have been uterus

mates, and they may even look the same, but they each have a unique character and will have different needs that must be met in different ways.

It won't take long for you to instinctively know what each twin requires at any given moment— knowledge that will have been acquired almost subconsciously in the process of surviving the first few days and weeks.

In the process of moving from feed to diaper change and back again, you will be constantly responding to the different needs of each baby and, in doing so, will be learning more about them and deepening your relationship with each twin without even realizing it.

You may worry that you do not love your babies equally—perhaps you find the less-demanding twin easier to love or perhaps you are drawn to the more challenging twin because calming them down gives you a sense of accomplishment? Try not to analyze or beat yourself up over the ebb and flow of your feelings. The behavior of both babies will change and change again, and although it may not always be comparable, your love will be equal.

You and your partner

Lack of sleep, stress, and little time for each other as a couple gives plenty of room for resentment and conflict to creep in to what is already a pressured environment. Communication, understanding, and appreciation for each other can all help diffuse the twin tension.

For the first few months it is unlikely you will want to do anything other than sleep the minute you crawl into bed, but a few kind words before you nod off can help remind you both that you and your partner are, in fact, on the same team.

Try to be tolerant and let the small stuff slide. Fatigue can make even the most mild-mannered grown-up grumpy, so it is unlikely either of you will be at your most considerate.

Soon after you come home from the hospital, your new twin chores will become apparent and you might want to consider sharing out duties so that work is divided as equally as possible. Perhaps introduce a currency of cuddling or cups of coffee if you would like to trade tasks, so that you keep the arrangement conducive to happiness. Consider having date nights, but instead of going out, you can stay in. Turn your phones off and the baby monitor on and eat a candle-lit prepared meal.

Twins come with lots of parenting positives; you each get a baby to cuddle with and you are both likely to be more involved in the day-to-day detail which enhances the likelihood of mutual understanding and, if all goes well, respect.

Siblings

Include siblings in the pregnancy so that they feel a part of it. Their age will dictate what is appropriate to share. Perhaps show them ultrasound pictures and get out their old baby photos.

Maybe older sibling(s) can help choose toys for the hospital or pick the outfits the babies will wear when they come home with you. It is a nice gesture to buy presents for big brothers or sisters from the babies to get things off to a good start.

Make sure that you arrange for the older child(ren) to stay with people they are comfortable with during emergencies and the birth itself.

Expect the older sibling(s) behavior to regress or deteriorate once the babies arrive and try not to radically change what is expected of them. Include them and encourage visitors to make a fuss of the other children in the house as well as the new babies.

Some children find the novelty of new babies exciting, but begin to resent them a few months later when they realize they are not going back! Be sensitive to the ongoing needs of your older children who will need reassurance and one-on-one time while you all adjust to your newly expanded family.

Going solo

There are more single women than ever wanting to conceive, as well as many other women going it alone for other reasons, so lone parenting is on the rise. Whether your journey as a multiple mom began as a solo experience or ended up that way, you will cope.

You will need a support network and it is worth getting regular help for as long as possible, but particularly in the first weeks when you return home.

It is true that newborns need constant love and care, but it doesn't always have to come from you. Give yourself permission to take a break, and then make sure you enjoy it. Ask family or friends, or a combination of the two, to watch the babies while you have some time out to relax and recharge. This is not a luxury, it is sanity survival!

You may feel as though life as a single parent to twins is a blur but you will gradually emerge from the sleepless fog of the early days and can proudly admire the family that you have nurtured.

Twin single mom Though hard work physically and emotionally, being a single parent can be very rewarding.

Dressing babies

Even the most experienced parent will only be able to dress one baby at a time, so savor the one-on-one time that dressing allows you to spend with each twin.

The basics

Most babies do not enjoy having clothes pulled over their heads, so choose styles with easy openings, such as snaps at the neck. Sing or talk to your babies and try to make the process as fun as possible—after all it is a skill you will need to use on a daily basis.

For the early days and weeks, sleep suits and onesies will be the easiest wardrobe choices. A long or short-sleeved onesie can be worn under a sleep suit. Onesies have snap fasteners which snap over the diaper, and sleep suits are all-in-one suits that cover the arms and legs (see p.41). The styles with snaps down the front are easiest to put on and take off, and ones with feet negate the need for socks, which rarely stay on for long! In the warmer months, footless sleep suits will help keep your babies cool.

Not too hot, not too cold

Do not assume that both babies will have the same wardrobe requirements. Some babies are naturally a little warmer or a little cooler, so check both twins' temperature rather than adopting a one-size-fits-both approach. Hats, cardigans, and blankets can be layered over the top of the base layers, depending on the weather. Newborn babies are not very good at regulating their temperature. It is important that they stay warm, but be aware that they can overheat under too many layers.

You can check your babies' temperatures by placing your hand on their tummies or the back of their necks. If it feels sweaty or unusually warm to you, then remove a layer of clothing or a blanket; if it feels cool, add a layer.

Sleep suits These are useful all-in-ones, and available in different styles to suit all kinds of weather.

Shoes

Once your twins begin to stand up and furniture-cruise around the room, you will know that walking is imminent. This can happen any time from nine to 18 months and when it does, it is important to have feet measured for correctly fitting shoes. Because your twins will continue to grow rapidly, you will need to have their feet measured roughly every six weeks to ensure that their shoes still fit.

The same or different

It is important to remember that even identical twins are not the same. There will be times when it is fun and festive to dress your babies the same or in a theme, and there will be days when the only clean clothes left are white sleep suits, but remember that your twins are individuals and you want people to respond to them as such. Eliminating confusion by dressing your twins differently can help you to learn the distinct character traits of your two babies.

You might want to consider coordinating outfits rather than matching—the same style in different colors perhaps. Save matching outfits for novelty occasions or commemorative photographs, but make sure you dress them differently in situations where you need to be certain other people can tell them apart, for relatives and babysitters for example.

If your twins are the same sex it may be easier to have communal clothes—it is not necessary to have separate wardrobes for each twin. Boy/girl twins may be able to share some basic items, which will save money and laundry time.

Stockpiling sizes

Check your drawers often since you will probably accumulate clothes in assorted sizes, and before you know it your teeny tiny babies will outgrow clothes that they've never worn. Once your babies have outgrown items take them out of circulation—it is frustrating to have nearly dressed your babies only to discover you can no longer fasten their outfits. Perhaps contact a local twins group to see if they would like some of your hand-me-downs for families who have just discovered their own double dose of baby news.

Beyond babies

By the end of the first year, you will find it hard to believe that your twins ever fit into doll-sized clothes. Some parents feel nostalgic folding away the sleep suits and hats that have been outgrown, but your babies' growing independence and mobility marks the start of some fun wardrobe choices. The bigger clothes that you dress them in are a reminder of their increasing independence and highlight your successes in safely getting everyone this far!

To each their own Even if you buy your babies the same clothes, consider dressing them in different colors.

Bathing, cleaning, and changing

Basic baby care can be time consuming and daunting in the early days, but remember that as each day passes, you will gain confidence in your new skills and get to know your babies better.

Diapers

Like it or not, as a twin mom you will become a diaper expert in no time, and with two babies, there is no excuse for partners, friends, and family to stay diaper novices either.

For the first few months your babies' diapers will need changing before or after every feeding, roughly every four hours, plus when they poop.

Disposable diapers are popular because of their convenience, but cloth diapers have come a long way and some companies offer a laundry service so, budget depending, you may not need to wash them yourself. There are also eco-friendly disposable diapers, so you can have the best of both worlds—look for fragrance-free diapers with biodegradable materials which will contain fewer chemicals.

Try to make changing-time fun: lavish attention and talk or sing to that baby. It is not their favorite part of the day either, so by making it as enjoyable as possible, you make life easier for everyone.

Always change your baby on a flat, sturdy surface, that is either at waist level or on the floor. Never leave them unattended. It can be helpful to have dedicated "diaper stations" that are always stocked with diapers, wipes, cream, and spare outfits. A waist-height change table is kinder to your back, but a wipe-clean mat on the floor is sufficient.

Diaper rash

Most babies' suffer from diaper rash at some point, but you can minimize the risks of skin irritation by changing frequently. Emollient creams can help prevent diaper rash and some diaper-free time that

Diaper change Clean your baby by gently lifting up her legs by her ankles and wiping down with a soft cotton pad or a cloth before you put on the new diaper.

allows fresh air onto the skin is advisable. If the skin is particularly sore and bleeding, contact your pediatrician who will advise you on how to treat it.

Bath time

Without the reassurance of a nurse to make sure you don't drop your slippery newborns, bathing at home can seem daunting, but practice makes perfect.

For the first few days you can gain confidence by sponge bathing your babies on a sturdy surface covered with a fluffy towel. Use warm, clean water and cotton pads to clean your babies' faces first, and then their bottoms. Use fresh water and cotton pads for each baby and make sure they do not get cold.

Baby baths come in different shapes and sizes and can be used before graduating to an adult-sized bath. Alternatively, you may want to use a bath seat in an adult bath, but make sure it is appropriate for newborns since many can be used only once a baby can support his or her own head.

Test the water with the inner part of your elbow; it should feel warm but not hot: 98°F (37°C) is about right. Babies scald more easily than children and grown-ups, and for extra reassurance you might want to invest in a baby bath thermometer.

Juggling bath towels and slippery babies can be a challenge. Towels that fasten around your neck like aprons, leaving both hands free to hold the baby close to you securely, are very handy for parents.

Do not bathe both babies together if you are by yourself. Make sure that the twin you are not bathing is left somewhere safe, perhaps in a bouncy seat and always within sight. You must never leave a baby unattended in the water and need to ensure their sibling is safe.

Have clean diapers and clothes ready so that when you have dried your baby, everything is already in place. Put the clean baby in the bouncy seat and you can bathe the other. It is not necessary to change the bath water unless the first baby has soiled it.

When your babies are small, it is not essential to bath them every day, but it can be a useful addition to your routine and signal a wind down to bed time. Every other day will suffice if you prefer to alternate bathing days.

Miniature manicures

Babies' nails grow quickly and can be very sharp. They will inadvertently scratch themselves while they learn to control their hands, so keeping nails trimmed is essential. Baby nail scissors are the right size for the job and a sleeping baby won't wiggle as much or object to waking with trimmed talons.

Bath basics Bath time for one baby means the other has to be secure in a seat and within your visual range.

Sleep

Fatigue comes with the twin territory, but you can help your babies to distinguish between night and day, and teach them to settle down themselves to sleep.

Cribs and co-sleeping

For reasons of space (and cuteness) you may initially want both babies to sleep in the same crib. It is important to use the feet-to-foot position in which babies' feet are right at the end of the crib to prevent them from wiggling under the covers (see p.43).

It may be tempting to snuggle up in your bed with the twins, but there is not enough evidence to be certain that co-sleeping with twins is safe. There is greater risk of overheating, and of someone falling out of bed. As a twin parent you are likely to be exceptionally tired, which can make you less likely to wake if you are in bed with your newborns and there is a problem. It is not sensible to co-sleep if you have been drinking, smoking, or are taking any medication.

A co-sleeping compromise is a pair of bassinets placed beside your bed. It ensures your babies are within arm's reach, but means you and your partner retain ownership of your bed. This setup means that your babies are close by for night feedings, which can help you benefit from a few minutes extra sleep.

Introducing a routine

Like all newborns, your babies will not initially know the difference between night and day (and after a few sleep-deprived weeks, neither will you!) but the good news is that you can gradually teach them. From around four months, your babies will be able to deal with longer periods between feedings and

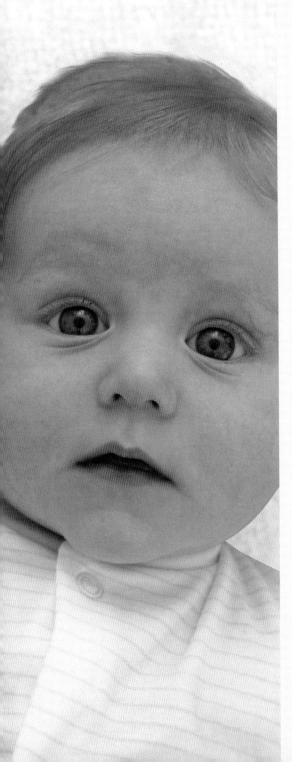

this may be a good time to introduce a simple, calming bedtime routine to help them to distinguish between day and night.

The word "routine" needn't be associated with strict rules and can be a gentle process that is repeated each day to establish boundaries and expectations. A twin routine may be harder to implement initially, but it is especially worthwhile so that everyone knows what to expect on a daily and nightly basis.

Introducing a nighttime routine will signal to your babies that it is time for sleep. You could consider a warm bath, massage, and quiet cuddling before putting them to bed. You can help your babies learn to fall asleep unaided by putting them down when they are drowsy but not asleep.

By setting a different mood during the night feedings—by keeping sound to a minimum, using low lighting, and not engaging in play—babies will learn that nighttime is for sleeping.

If you are breast-feeding, consider expressing milk during the day (see p.81) so that your partner can help you by bottle-feeding one baby at night. You can alternate who is given the breast and who is given the bottle at each feeding. If you are using formula, make sure that you have enough sterilized bottles before you go to bed to keep things as stress-free as possible in the small hours.

As they get bigger, your babies are more likely to disturb each other if they are sharing a crib. It is best to plan for two cribs by the time they are three months, when they could begin to roll over. Current guidelines suggest that parents have their infants in the same room as them for six months. If space prohibits this, make sure you have, and use, a baby monitor and check the batteries regularly.

Sleep patterns Both babies may not adapt to your bedtime routine immediately but with some discipline from you, both will soon know that night is for sleeping.

The year ahead

Your babies will be "jet lagged" for the first few days and may surprise you by sleeping through rounds of rowdy visitors. Then they will become increasingly alert and their sleeping patterns may vary. For example, one twin may be more prone to gas, making him or her harder to settle down after a night feeding. However tempting it is to climb back into your bed at the first opportunity, it is worthwhile taking a few moments to make sure both babies have been burped and are comfortable since they will sleep longer.

How well your babies sleep is often weight-rather than age-dependent, but temperament is also a strong influencing factor so, even when your babies are a similar weight, they may have varying sleep patterns. As you get to know your twins you will learn how best to settle each baby down. It is worthwhile trying to get them on a similar schedule.

Some babies are naturally better sleepers than others and you may find that one twin settles more easily. Remember that your babies are two individuals and their distinct personalities will inevitably mean that you cannot always adopt a one-size-fits-all sleep policy, but there are things you can do to encourage both to sleep well.

Swaddling Swaddling is an age-old custom whereby babies are wrapped snugly in a cotton sheet or specially-made piece of fabric that can help them feel safe and secure. Before babies learn to control their limbs they can inadvertently keep themselves awake with jerky movements. By restricting their movement, they will stay still and calm. It does not work for all babies, but you may want to try it (see below).

1 Lay your baby on a blanket folded triangularly, with the head slightly above the blanket line. Tuck in the arms lightly before you go to Step 2.

2 Gently pull one side of the blanket across and tuck it under your baby's side. You can tuck in the arms entirely or leave a little room for movement.

3 Tuck the other side of the blanket in the same way as the first. Your baby is now swaddled and can be laid on his back in the crib to sleep.

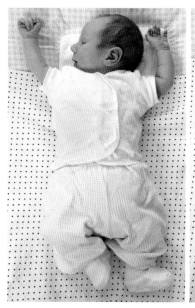
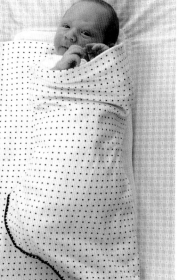
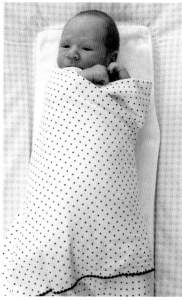

Self-soothing Some babies fuss for a while when they are put in their cribs, but give them a chance to settle down. Offer reassurance by stroking faces and tummies. It is not always necessary to take them out of the crib to calm them and the sleeping twin won't necessarily wake when their sibling is being noisy. By providing reassurance without taking your babies out of the crib you are teaching them tools to soothe themselves.

If both babies wake simultaneously, it is tempting to attend to the twin that is crying the loudest first, but by doing so you reinforce that the louder the volume, the quicker the response. By tending to the quieter twin first, you reinforce the notion that response is not volume-dependent.

Sleep synchronicity If one baby wakes for a feeding, consider waking the other. Although it can seem counterintuitive to wake a sleeping baby, it may be the only way to get them on a similar schedule and ensure you get some time to rest, otherwise it is likely that one or other baby will be awake most or all of the time. Do not despair if things unravel just when you thought you were making progress. It may sometimes feel like one sleep step forward and two tired ones back but week by week you will all be making progress.

Sofa snoozing It can be tempting, when sleep deprivation accumulates, to doze on the sofa with your newborns, but this can be potentially dangerous since your babies could become wedged down the back of the sofa, or between you and the couch.

Moses baskets are a very portable way of keeping your babies near you while they (and you) nap during the day. It is not advisable to put both babies in one basket, except for photo opportunities, since they may overheat. It is not worthwhile spending a lot of money on Moses baskets because your babies will outgrow them very quickly.

Naps Your babies will spend much of their first few days and weeks sleeping, gradually becoming more alert for longer periods. By six months your babies will probably be having a morning and afternoon nap. This pattern will continue until they approach their second birthday, when it is likely that they will have one longer nap in the middle of the day.

Some moms like to be more prescriptive than others about when their babies sleep and enforce naps at set times, the advantage being that you know when during the day you will have some twin-free time. However you organize things, it is tempting, especially in the early days, to want to catch up on housework and other chores while your babies are asleep, but remember that it is important for you to rest, too.

If your babies are tired but refusing to settle down consider a change of scene, bundle everyone up in the stroller and go for a walk. The fresh air and exercise can be good for your mood and the motion often helps to settle little ones down.

Doctor's advice

Sudden Infant Death Syndrome (SIDS)

SIDS is the unexplained death of a baby. It occurs most often under the age of four months, but can happen to older babies. Although not entirely preventable, changing the way that babies sleep has helped to reduce the toll—and the heartbreak that accompanies SIDS. Some of the risk factors for SIDS, such as prematurity and low birth weight, mean that twins could be at greater risk. In addition to following guidelines on safe sleeping, always seek medical advice if you think one of your twins is not well.

Crying

Newborn babies are unable to do anything for themselves and cry to communicate a need. As you get to know your twins, you will quickly learn to determine what that need is.

Twin tears

All babies cry and, at times, all parents find it hard to deal with. Your twins may cry for different reasons, and some babies naturally do it more than others. You may know that one twin is upset, in need, or feeling ill if they are unusually loud, whereas the other signals that something is wrong by being unusually quiet. Twins will cry for the same reasons singleton babies do. So, when one or both start to cry, think if one of the following could be the reason why.

Hunger A baby's small stomach cannot hold very much food, which is why they need to be fed little and often. If your babies are crying, they may be hungry, so offer them some milk. They may not stop crying immediately, but give them time to continue feeding, either breast or bottle, since they may be soothed as their stomachs fill.

Discomfort If your babies have recently been fed and continue to cry, they may be uncomfortable. Trapped gas can be painful for babies and they need to be burped in order to release it. Patting or rubbing your babies' backs is the most effective way to bring up gas and ease the discomfort.

Bawling Every cry isn't an emergency, but it isn't without reason either. In time, you'll know what their cries are for.

Dirty diaper Some babies tolerate dirty diapers, whereas others protest as soon as theirs become full. Urine and feces can irritate tender skin, so regular changes are important to keep diaper rash at bay.

Ambient temperature Newborns often cry when you bathe them or change their diaper because they object to the cool air on their skin. You will soon become efficient at changes and your babies will be clean and warm in no time.

Body temperature Babies' hands and feet are often cool because they are not very good at regulating their temperature. Feel your babies' stomachs or the back of their necks to see that they feel warm but not too hot, sweaty, cool, or clammy. Add or remove layers accordingly.

Fatigue Babies can often become overly stimulated, which makes it hard for them to shut down. You can help them to rest by creating a calm, quiet, and dark environment that is conducive to sleep.

Boredom After the first three months, your babies may need to be stimulated. Toys, mobiles, crinkly books, or you singing can all cheer up your babies.

Contact The arrival of twins was a shock to you, but imagine how shocked your babies were to leave the comfort of their cosy home! They may be reassured by the sound of your heartbeat, so hold them close. Your babies may prefer you to move around with them because before birth there would have been constant movement, so this will be familiar to them.

No reason at all If you have checked all of the above and your babies are still crying, then consider bundling them up and going out for a walk. A change of scenery, some fresh air, and the motion of the stroller can help to restore calm.

Doctor's advice

When is crying a symptom of illness?

Most of the time, your twins aren't crying because they're sick, but when they are ill it's vital to recognize the clues. A baby may vomit, have frequent runny stools, or refuse a feeding. Feel your baby's skin. Cold or clammy skin suggests something is wrong, especially if there's mottling or any other color changes.

Check for signs of dehydration, such as loose, dry-feeling skin and a sunken fontanelle (see p.77). These are linked with a serious lack of fluid. An earlier sign is finding that a baby's diapers are dry when you might expect them to be wet.

Look out, also, for rapid breathing or breathlessness, or anything else that appears unusual. If you suspect one of your babies is ill, talk to your pediatrician without delay and learn to trust your instincts.

Time for a cuddle Sometimes babies cry because they just want to be held and be in contact with you.

At home

The modifications you need to make to your home will change as your babies get older. Simple steps can keep your babies safe and your house intact.

Early days

When you bring your newborns home from the hospital, you will want to make sure that your home is safe. The first thing you can do is make sure that there are no trip hazards—your babies may not be able to move far initially but you will be carrying them around and fatigue is likely to make you clumsier and less observant than normal.

Make sure nothing is left on the stairs and consider installing new light bulbs so you know halls, stairs, and landings will be well lit when you need them to be. Put nonslip pads under any rugs and mats that don't already have nonslip backs, and keep floors free of clutter.

Baby proofing Insert socket covers over electrical sockets to prevent your curious babies from sticking their fingers or small objects into the holes.

If you assembled nursery furniture way back at the beginning of your pregnancy, give everything a once over before you use it for the first time. Check that spare parts and empty packaging have been removed and stored out of harm's way.

Finger friendly

It will be hard to imagine when your two little bundles are still small, but by the end of their first year they will be on the move and looking for trouble. Beware of toilet seats and trunks with lids that can slam down on little fingers. Put safety covers in all unused electrical outlets and install hinge protectors on cupboards and drawers.

Out of reach Store all medicines and potentially harmful items in a locked cabinet or on a high shelf since babies tend to put most things in their mouths.

Out of reach

It is preferable to have curtains and blinds without cords, but if you do have them, make sure they are up high and out of reach. Tie them in a knot or put up a hook that you can wrap them around securely. Loose cords are a strangulation risk.

Move hazardous items, such as bleach, to high cupboards and keep knives in locked drawers. Stationery items such as pens, scissors, and paperclips all pose risks, so keep them out of reach in a pot or other container.

Be alert to dangers in wastebaskets and trash containers around the house. Consider the potential risk of what is being discarded; batteries, old razors, lengths of dental floss, and other household waste should not be left within reach of inquisitive twins.

Furniture, windows, and doors

Hide appliance cords behind heavy furniture and be aware of items that could topple over. Bolt bookshelves and bureaus to the wall and make sure televisions are secure.

Put colorful stickers on glass doors and tables to prevent bumps. Put corner protectors on all furniture with sharp corners. Put locks on low windows so they cannot be opened further than is safe.

Babies scald easily, so make sure radiators are covered, and remind family and guests not to drink or leave hot beverages near your twins.

A safe place

If the phone rings or the doorbell sounds, it will not always be possible to take both babies with you. Having a travel crib, play pen, or bouncy seat nearby provides a safe place for you to leave increasingly mobile babies while you have to briefly go out of sight. Check playpens and travel cribs often to make sure they are correctly and securely assembled and that nothing hazardous has dropped into them.

Out of sight If you have to leave your babies briefly unattended always make sure they are safe.

Smoke and fire

Install smoke alarms and check them regularly to make sure they are working. If you have a fireplace, install a fixed fireguard and keep an extinguisher nearby. Do not put items that will appeal to your twins on the mantelpiece or around the fire.

First aid

Common sense, precautions, supervision, and vigilance are the best accident-prevention tools, but it is sensible to be prepared in the event of an accident. Have a well-stocked first-aid kit in your home, keep it out of reach of your babies, but make sure all those left in charge know where it is kept.

Outings and vacations

It won't take long for you to learn the baby care basics and you will soon have the confidence to take your new family out of the house.

Packing a diaper bag

In addition to your babies, there are a few other things you need to take with you when you and your new family go out and about. It is sensible to keep a diaper bag packed with the basics so you know you are good to go whenever the mood takes you.

When looking to buy a diaper bag, consider two-in-one designs—that way you only have to clip one bag to your stroller but have a bag for each baby. One large bag is adequate, but can leave you rummaging around when you need to locate something. Separate bags also mean your partner or a friend can take a bag and a baby, which can speed things up if both babies need changing together.

The exact contents of your diaper bag will depend on your babies, the weather, and the nature and duration of your outing, but the following list should get you started:

- disposable changing mat
- six diapers
- package of wipes
- small container of diaper cream
- plastic bags to dispose of dirty diapers
- changes of clothes for the babies
- four cans of prepared formula
- two sterilized bottles
- two burp cloths
- some appropriate toys
- a spare top for you—just in case!

You will need to check the contents of your bag regularly since your babies will grow quickly and may outgrow items in the bag. It is good practice to stock up the bag again each time you return home in case you need to leave in a hurry the next time you depart.

Packing up Having a designated diaper bag packed with all the items you may need when out and about makes it easier to leave the house with your babies.

You may be intimidated by the thought of leaving the house with your twins, but a change of scenery will be good for you all, so your efforts will be rewarded.

First outings

Your first outings are likely to be to the pediatrician for checkups. These are great for building confidence since they are usually local and you know that you will have the support of trained staff there if you run into problems or have any questions. As a "multiple mom" you may be in the minority at your doctor's, but the admiring glances you get from moms with a single baby will do you the world of good. Yes, you do deserve a hug and a pat on the back for getting your new brood out of the house.

Further afield

Traveling with twins can be an intimidating prospect and for many the suggestion of a vacation sounds more like a headache. Extended time away from home or a long-haul trip requires planning, but the following suggestions might help make your time away memorable for the right reasons.

Plan for the worse-case scenario—and then be pleasantly surprised! Pack quantities of diapers, food, and clothes on the assumption that your mode of transportation will be delayed. That way you can be certain to have enough to tide you over until you arrive at your destination.

Double up If you are traveling with a partner or friend, consider leaving the deluxe tandem stroller at home and buying two cheap, collapsible single strollers. These will fit through all doorways and make getting around easier.

Flying It is safe for babies to fly, but they can find the pressure change on takeoff and landing uncomfortable. Feed them or give them a pacifier to suck during takeoff and landing to help minimize the chance of ear-related discomfort.

Inform your airline that you will be traveling with twins. Check to see if there are airline-provided bassinets, or sky cribs, available for your babies. If you are traveling with older babies, check the seating rules: some airlines only allow one baby per aisle and you will want to book your tickets accordingly.

Heading out Leaving the house with your twins takes a bit of planning but a change of scenery and some fresh air will benefit you all.

Starting twins on solids

The introduction of solid food to a baby's diet is a process. Initially your babies will prefer bland, smooth foods but their tastes will become increasingly adventurous as they grow.

More than milk

The early days and nights that you spent worrying about feeding your babies on bottle or breast milk may seem like dim and distant memories now that you have gained confidence and established a routine that works for you. Unfortunately, like so many areas of parenting, just when you feel you've got the hang of something that was challenging, it is time to learn and deal with the next challenge… enter solids!

Solids basics Your babies cannot chew right away, so their first solid food will have to be puréed; you can prepare purée in advance and freeze it.

As with all new parenting skills, it is sensible not to put too much pressure on yourself, or your babies. Starting solids is a process and there is no one-size-fits-all rule. The first stages are about getting babies to try tiny tastes of new foods—there is no need to rush things. You may want to start with just one solid meal a day. There is no need to worry too much about your babies having a balanced diet initially since they will still be getting most of their nutrition from milk. Milk will continue to be an important part of your babies' diet until they are at least 12 months, but gradually their diet becomes more substantial and they will drink less milk.

Continuing to feed your babies milk, either breast or bottle, will help them through the transitional period and provide them with the comfort and physical closeness that they have come to associate with being fed. Milk feedings will decrease gradually as their consumption of solid food increases.

When to start solids

A baby's digestive system is usually too immature to deal with anything other than milk before they reach four months. Speak to your pediatrician if for some reason you think your babies need to start earlier than this.

From four to six months, your babies will have the head control and the digestive enzymes required to deal with food. Their kidneys are ready and their jaws and tongues have developed enough to manage eating and swallowing foods. If you wait much longer than six months to start solids, your babies may be more resistant. They need to develop a liking for different foods, so by waiting you risk prolonging the process.

If your babies were premature, talk to your doctor about when to start solids. Some very premature babies may not be ready for solid foods at 6 months. Parents should discuss with their doctor whether the baby is ready for solids based on developmental milestones such as head control, nutritional needs, and how much milk they are drinking.

Spotting the signs

Your twins won't necessarily be ready for solids at exactly the same time but look for the following signs that indicate a readiness for solids:

- no longer seem content after a full feeding
- hungry within three hours of the last feeding
- start to wake at night having previously slept through
- show an interest in food and people eating
- chew fists and fingers

How to start solids Starting can be broken into three stages with different foods and textures being appropriate at each stage. Here are some ideas:

Stage one (around 6 months)

- Semiliquid purées
- Baby rice; bananas; avocado; apple; melon; potato; turnip; carrot; butternut squash; pumpkin

Stage two (around 6–9 months)

- Thicker purées and soft finger foods
- Berries; dried apricots; plums; spinach; corn; zucchini; broccoli; bread; couscous; pasta; well-cooked fish, well-cooked meat, and eggs; hard pasteurized cheese; whole-milk plain yogurt; cow's milk (both in cooking and with cereal); butter

Fickle foodies Some babies are reluctant to try new foods, but remember there is no need to rush. A food rejected one day may be a real favorite the next.

Stage three (around 10–12 months)

• Chopped, mashed, minced, and lumpy foods; hard finger foods

• Citrus fruit; dried fruit; soft pasteurized cheese and additional vegetables; grains and proteins to broaden your babies' repertoire

Convenience and cost

It is convenient and more cost-effective to make up batches of food and freeze them. Defrost a small amount and heat up only what you think might be consumed. Your twins may exhibit a preference for different foods, but do not be deterred if your babies reject a purée one week—they may want seconds the following week!

Some moms have mixed feelings about their babies being ready for solid food and feel nostalgic for the teeny tiny baby days. It is a big change for your babies, too, so go slowly and give yourself all the time you need to adjust.

One spoon or two

Most twin moms will admit to using one spoon to feed both babies, since having separate utensils can mean meal times last forever. You might, however, like to consider using a separate bowl for each twin so that you know how much each has had to eat.

As your babies grow, you may want to give them their own bowl and spoon to play with. They are unlikely to be very efficient at first, but allowing them to play and try to feed themselves is all part of the process.

Multiple mess

Solids are messy, and with two babies things can get very messy indeed—especially when they want to feed themselves. Set meal times up on

Variety is the spice For all-around development, make sure that your babies eat a wide variety of foods, since different foods provide different health benefits.

easy-to-clean floors or place newspaper or a sheet of plastic under your babies' highchairs. Be prepared to wipe down doors and walls—and even ceilings! To minimize the number of outfits you get through in one day, perhaps you could invest in bibs or plastic aprons that can be put on over your twins' clothes and wiped down after each meal.

Diaper surprises

By changing what goes in to your babies' bodies, you inevitably change what comes out! Their diapers may now be full of surprises as you introduce their bodies to different foods. Be aware of the foods that can cause constipation, including apples and bananas. Consider adding some cooled boiled water to your babies' diets if you think they are prone to constipation.

Try and try again Encourage your babies to try and feed themselves. It may be messy at first, but they will enjoy it, and it will help their manual dexterity.

Doctor's advice

Vitamins and supplements

Most of your babies' nutrition should come from food, not out of the medicine cabinet. But vitamin drops are important because babies don't always get enough. While babies with good appetites and a varied diet are less likely to need supplements, they can be short. Vitamin D is particularly crucial in northern regions as well as for babies with darker skin who do not absorb as much vitamin D from the sun.

Babies who are breast-fed exclusively need a vitamin D supplement of 400 IU a day, because breast milk does not have enough of the vitamin to meet your babies' needs. Vitamin D is added to formula, so most formula-fed babies do not need a supplement. Your babies may need a larger supplement if they are premature or if you live in a northern community (north of 55° latitude, which is about the level of Edmonton). A larger dose will need to be prescribed, so check with your doctor about your babies' specific needs.

Don't give your babies other vitamin or mineral supplements unless they are recommended by your doctor. They will not make your twins healthier or more intelligent unless they definitely lack a nutrient. Iron is especially toxic to youngsters so avoid iron supplements unless your doctor gives them to you, and stick to the prescribed amount.

Keeping your babies healthy

There's a lot you can do to keep your twins healthy and to manage more easily with any minor illnesses that may crop up during their first year.

Checkups

After the first checkup when they enter the world, your twins' next visit with a doctor is usually within a week or two of your discharge from the hospital to check that your babies are gaining weight and for the doctor to answer any questions that new moms and dads usually have. Their next full medical exam is usually at around one to two months when your family doctor or pediatrician examines your babies fully and asks how you and they are doing. Pediatric practices may differ slightly in the frequency of their suggested visits but most babies are seen at least every other month for the first six months, then every three months until they are about 18 months, when the visits become less frequent. All visits to the doctor involve the baby being weighed and measured, as well as a physical exam and evaluation of developmental milestones. Babies will also receive routine vaccinations at some visits, and parents should be given an opportunity to ask questions about things like feeding, sleep, development or any other issue they have.

Keeping infections at bay

Most moms know that an ultraclean environment isn't ideal for a baby's developing immune system. On the other hand, babies are vulnerable to infection, and common bacteria and viruses can make them very ill. That's why you need to sterilize everything that enters your new babies' mouths, though not everything they come into contact with. Pay

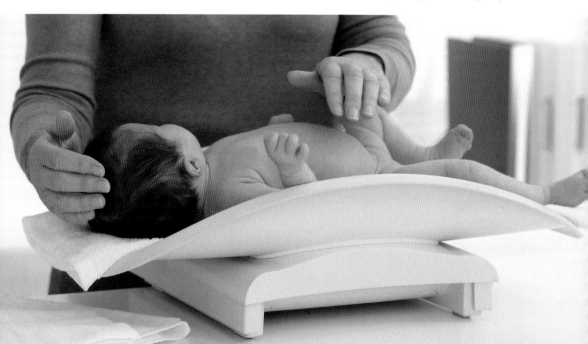

Weighing Twins will need to be weighed every so often, but not necessarily every week. Ask your pediatrician.

particular attention to pacifiers, bottles, nipples, and other feeding equipment. As they progress through this first year, you can become a little less fastidious. By the time your twins are six months old, it is often enough just to put dishes and spoons in the dishwasher. Because twins share the same germs, you can use the same spoon for both babies, unless your doctor advises otherwise.

Pets can be a bonus for a baby's health and development, but keep your dog or cat healthy and follow simple hygiene precautions. Fluffy or Rover should not share your babies' bedroom, and you must prevent your twins from investigating the contents of the cat's litter box.

When they are ill

Most illnesses are likely to be minor, but babies can and do get ill. You will soon develop an instinct for when one or other twin isn't well. With two babies of the same age, you also have a handy benchmark for the feel of the skin, normal behavior, bowel actions, and sometimes appetite (but twins can differ).

Even though twins share many germs, they don't always become ill at the same time. Always treat each twin separately. They should have separate health records and their own prescriptions, even when they are both given the same medicine.

It can be hard taking sick babies to the doctor. When you need to go there, warn the receptionist that you will need help. They should try to fit your babies in without a wait and be ready to offer you a hand, too.

It's tough taking care of sick babies and even minor illnesses can be a struggle at times. Make sure you get as much rest as you can, and take any offers of help from family, friends, and neighbors. If only one of your babies is sick, maybe a friend can help take care of the other one for just a couple of hours until you return from the pediatrician's office.

Doctor's advice

Immunizations

Immunization is the most effective way of preventing your twins from catching serious infections, and the routine schedule provided by your doctor is designed to maximize the protection a baby gets from each vaccine. If your twins were born pre-term, immunizations should still be done at the usual intervals, starting at about six weeks from birth. If you can, get help from your partner or a relative for the evening after any immunization, since it can be hard soothing two fractious babies at once. If this is impossible, you may want to immunize your twins on different days. But it is not advisable to split up the vaccines or deviate too far from the schedule.

Getting the needle Hold each baby gently but firmly, and consider offering a breast-feeding or pacifier right after the injection.

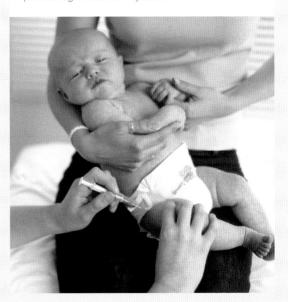

The first birthday

Congratulations, you made it! Your first year as a twin parent was no doubt as challenging as it was wonderful, so mark the special occasion, but don't create unnecessary stress for yourself.

Small and successful

Birthdays are milestones and have extra significance for twins because they are a reminder of the very special bond they share. Birthday parties are one of the few occasions when you can save money: there is only one venue and one set of invitations! However, your one year olds may be unsettled by a large gathering, so don't feel obligated to organize an ambitious event—it may not have the desired effect.

It is important to make sure each twin feels special and unique, but children can get overly excited and overly tired at birthday parties, so keep things simple; limit the number of guests and make sure the venue is childproof and age appropriate.

Guests will wonder what the correct gift etiquette is for twins; the answer will depend on the babies in question. If you know that life is easier with identical toys, then let it be known. Perhaps "the same, but different" works best in your house? You will have to live with the consequences of present envy, so make life as straightforward as possible and communicate your wishes. Let it be known that the twins would appreciate a present each, unless it is a play item made for multiple users, such as a sand box or a ball pool. Friends and family will appreciate the guidance.

Cupcakes are a good solution to the "one cake or two" twin-birthday dilemma and you can decide whether to sing one round of Happy Birthday or two. Consider asking a friend or family member to take photos for you—that way you can make sure the day runs smoothly, safe in the knowledge that it is being captured for posterity.

Reflection and recognition

Your babies may have grown significantly over the past 12 months, but they are still too small to fully appreciate what is going on around them and, after all your hard work, it is really you who deserves a party! Sleep deprivation may have stolen memories of the first few months, so this is a great time for reflection. Acknowledge and reward your achievements over the past year.

During year one, Team Twin probably included friends and family members, and you might want to use the first birthday as a chance to thank them for their support.

Your family, babies, and body have all changed significantly over the last year and you can feel proud of all of them for getting this far.

Your life will now be forever split into pre-twin or post-twin segments and you can be the voice of authority for others who are expecting twins. In the process of imparting your wisdom, you will realize just how much you have learned and this should give you confidence as you embark on the second year of your life-long twin journey. You have all reached a new kind of normal; you have adjusted to being Mom and can now change diapers and pack a diaper bag without a moment's hesitation. You may not notice day by day how much you have all learned but the first birthday is a great excuse to look back and admire your accomplishments.

Milestone This is a special day for all of you, so do not overburden yourself; if a big party means more work for you and less time with your twins, keep it small and cosy.

Resources

Resources for parents of twins:

Marvelous Multiples
Resources for a multiple pregnancy.
www.marvelousmultiples.com

Multiple Birth: Prenatal Information and Bereavement Support
Pregnancy and postnatal information for parents of multiples.
www.multiplebirthsfamilies.com

Multiple Births Canada
Support for parents who are expecting multiples.
www.multiplebirthscanada.org

Pregnancy:

Babycenter Canada
Information on conception, pregnancy, and birth; free e-newletters and forums.
www.babycenter.ca

Canada's Food Guide
Information on healthy eating.
www.hc-sc.gc.ca/fn-an/food-guide-aliment/index-eng.php

The Childbirth Experience
Services and resources for families involved in higher-risk pregnancies.
www.childbirthexperience.ca

Motherisk
Information on the safety of medications, infections, and chemicals during pregnancy and breast-feeding.
www.motherisk.org

Preeclampsia Foundation
Information and support for those with preeclampsia.
www.preeclampsia.org

Society of Obstetricians and Gynaecologists of Canada
www.sogc.org

Labor and birth:

Canadian Association of Midwives
Find a midwife in your area.
www.canadianmidwives.org

Childbirth and Postpartum Professional Association
Find childbirth educators, lactation consultants, and doulas in your area.
www.cappacanada.ca

Lamaze International
Information about the Lamaze approach to pregnancy and birth.
www.lamaze.org

After the birth:

About Kids Health
Trusted answers from The Hospital for Sick Children.
www.aboutkidshealth.ca

Caring for Kids
Children's health information from the Canadian Paediatric Society.
www.caringforkids.cps.ca

La Leche League Canada
Support for breast-feeding moms.
www.lllc.ca

Safe Kids Canada
Information about child safety at home and elsewhere.
www.safekidscanada.ca

Support groups:

Autism Society Canada
www.autismsocietycanada.ca

Canadian Cystic Fibrosis Foundation
www.cysticfibrosis.ca

Canadian Diabetes Association
www.diabetes.ca

Canadian Down Sydrome Society
www.cdss.ca

Canadian Foundation for the Study of Sudden Infant Death
www.sidscanada.org

Rights and benefits:

Canada Child Tax Benefit
www.servicecanada.gc.ca/eng/goc/cctb.shtml

Employment Insurance Maternity and Parental Benefits
www.servicecanada.gc.ca/eng/sc/ei/benefits/maternityparental.shtml

Quebec Parental Insurance Plan
www.rqap.gouv.qc.ca/index_en.asp

Index

A

ability differences 95
acetaminophen 32, 33
air travel 115
alcohol 15, 49, 82–83
amniocentesis 30, 31
amniotic fluid 25, 26, 30, 64, 69
    excess 37, 60
    water breaking 55, 68
amniotic sac 13, 16, 26
    shared 29
analgesics 33
anatomy scan 29, 30
anemia 23, 29
ankles, puffy 51
antacids 33
amniocentesis 30, 31
    blood tests 28, 29
    chorionic villus sampling (CVS) 30–31
    ultrasound scans 24, 26, 28, 29, 30
    urine tests 31, 37
amniotomy 68
aspirin 33
au pairs 87

B

baby monitors 43, 108
baby talk 96
baby nurses 87
backaches 34, 56
bath water temperature 105
bathing 45, 104–105
belly bands 21
belly growth 20, 22–23
birth
    delivery 56–57
    due date 54
    forceps delivery 59, 62, 67, 69
    home birth 63
    hospital birth 62–63
    labor stages 56–57
    labor symptoms 54–56
    people present 62
    vacuum delivery 62, 67, 69
    see also cesarean (C-section);
        vaginal delivery
birth plan 40, 48, 58–59
birth weight 13
birthdays 122
bleeding 33, 36
    "bloody show" 55
blood tests 28, 29
"bloody show" 55
blurred vision 36, 37
body temperature 76, 102, 111

bonding
    belated 79
    in the uterus 26
    kangaroo care (skin-to-skin care) 89
    one-on-one time 78–79
    twin bonding 26, 98
    with newborns 78–79, 89, 99
bottle-feeding
    combination feeding 83, 84, 107
    equipment 45, 84
    formula 84
    making up feedings 84
    supporting your babies 85
    tandem feeding 85
bouncy seats 44–45
boy-girl twins 12, 29
bras 21, 23, 40
Braxton-Hicks contractions 55
breast changes 23
breast pads 40, 80
breast pumps 81, 82
breast-feeding 80–83
    after a cesarean 72
    benefits 81, 83
    combination feeding 83, 84, 107
    cushion support 44, 72, 83
    diet and 82–83
    expressing milk 45, 81, 82, 89
    in public 83
    latching on 80, 82
    little and often 81
    mastitis 83
    on demand 81
    same breast/same child 81
    separate feeding 80
    tandem feeding 80–81, 83
breech position 55, 64, 65, 68, 69
burp cloths 41

C

cesarean (C-section) 57, 63, 64, 65, 70–73
    birth plan 58–59
    emergency cesarean 69, 70
    emotions 73
    pain relief 67, 70
    planned (elective) cesarean 67, 70
    procedure 70–71
    recovery from 18, 72–73
    stitching 71
    vaginal birth after cesarean (VBAC)
        73
car seats 42
carpal tunnel syndrome (CTS) 34–35
cephalic presentation 64, 65
cerebral palsy 61
changing stations 43, 104
childbirth classes 46–7
chorionic membranes 28, 29

chorionic villus sampling (CVS) 30–31
chromosomal disorders 31
cleft lip 30
clothes 102–103
    communal 103
    dressing babies 102–103
    individuality 76, 77
    maternity wear 20, 21
coffee, and breast-feeding 82
comparisons, avoiding 95
concerns and fears, voicing 29, 37, 46, 47,
    48
constipation 19, 33
    babies 119
contractions 54, 55, 57, 63, 66
cooperative play 98
cord prolapse 55, 70, 73
cramps 35
crawling 94, 95
crib bedding 43
crib death see Sudden Infant Death
    Syndrome (SIDS)
cribs 43, 106, 107
crying 110–111
cystic fibrosis 31

D

deep vein thrombosis (DVT) 72
dehydration
    babies 77, 111
    mother 14, 61
developmental stages 94–98
diaper bags 114
diapers 41, 104
    changing 104, 111
    disposables 104
diaper rash 104, 111
dichorionic (DC) twins 29
diet and breast-feeding 82, 83
    food hygiene 15, 50
    pregnancy 14–15
    supplements 15
dilation of the cervix 56, 69
dizygotic (DZ) twins see nonidentical
    (fraternal) twins
doulas 87
Down syndrome 28, 29, 31
drugs
drug issues 49, 60
    prescription 33

E

electrical safety 112
electronic fetal monitoring 62, 68
embryos 24
emotions 48–49, 56, 73, 89
epidurals 66–67, 69, 70, 72
estimated due date (EDD) 54
ethnicity 12

Index

exercise
    after birth 18–19
    at work 34, 51
    benefits 19
    daily life activities 19
    during pregnancy 16–19
    stretching exercises 17, 18, 34, 35, 51
    when not to 18, 19

F

falls 16, 18
family history of twins 12
fatigue 32, 35, 37
feeding 80–85
    logging times and amounts 45, 85
    nighttime feedings 107
    premature babies 61, 80, 88, 89
    solids 116–119
    vitamin and mineral supplements 119
    see also bottle-feeding; breast-feeding
fentanyl 66
fertility treatments 12
fetal alcohol syndrome 15
fetal development 24–26
fetal distress 57, 69, 70, 73
fetal fibronectin 61
fibroids 64
fire safety 113
first-aid kit 113
first trimester 11, 20, 23, 24, 36
fluid retention 34, 36
folic acid 15, 23
fontanelles 77, 111
food hygiene 15, 50
forceps delivery 59, 62, 67, 69
fraternal twins see nonidentical
    (fraternal) twins
fundus 22

G

gas 108, 110
gender of your babies, finding out 24, 31
general anesthesia 59, 70, 72
gestational diabetes 19, 37
glucose tolerance test 37

H

hats 41
head shapes 77
headaches 32, 34, 35, 36
heart rate in pregnancy 23
heartbeat, babies' 24, 62, 68
heartburn 33
hemorrhoids 33
herbal remedies 33
high blood pressure 19, 36, 37
home birth 63
hospital bags
    babies 41

mother 40
hospital birth 62–63
housework 19, 20, 87
hunger 110
hydramnios 37
hydration 14, 16, 17, 18, 35, 50, 83

I

ibuprofen 33, 61
identical twins 12, 13, 95
    dressing 76, 77, 102–103
    monochorionic (MC) twins 29
    size and weight 94
illnesses 120–121
immunizations 121
in vitro fertilization (IVF) 10, 12
individuals, treating twins as 13, 77, 95,
    96, 97, 98, 99, 102–103
induction 68
infections 120–121
insomnia 19
interest in twins 49, 114–115
intraventricular hemorrhage 61
iron supplements 23, 119

K

kangaroo care (skin-to-skin care) 89

L

labor
    inducing 68
    pain relief 57, 58, 59, 63, 66–67
    premature 15, 60, 61
    stages of 56–57
    symptoms 54–56
labor and delivery nurses 62, 63
language acquisition 96
lanugo 25
laxatives 33
learning experiences 94
leggings 21

M

magnesium sulphate 61
mastitis 83
maternity leave and benefits 51
maternity pads 40
maternity tanks 21
maternity wear 20, 21
meconium 25, 69
medical checkups 120
medications 33
membrane rupture 55, 60
milk banks 80
miscarriage 11, 15, 36
monochorionic (MC) twins 29, 30,
    37, 57
monochorionic monoamniotic (MCMA)
    twins 29

monozygotic twins (MZ) see identical
    twins
Montgomery's tubercles 23
morning sickness 32
morphine 66
Moses baskets 109
mother's helpers 87
muscular dystrophy 31
music 58, 59

N

nails, trimming 105
names, using 96
nannies 87
naps 109
nausea 32
Neonatal Intensive Care Unit (NICU) 88
nesting activities 19, 54
newborn babies 76–77
    appearance 76, 77
    bonding with 78–79, 89, 99
    head shapes 77
    nifedipine 61
    nonidentical (fraternal) twins 12, 13,
        94, 95
nitrous oxide 66, 67
nuchal translucency 28, 29, 30
nursery 43, 112
nursing bras 23, 40
nursing chairs 43
nutrition see diet

O

oblique presentation 64
one-on-one time 96, 99
onesies 41, 102
outings and vacations 114–115
overstimulation 111
oxytocin 68, 69

P

pain relief 57, 58, 59, 63, 66–67, 69, 70, 72
parallel play 98
parental leave and benefits 51
parenting classes 47
partner
    at the birth 58, 59, 68, 70, 71, 72
    attending childbirth classes 47
    bonding with the babies 79
    healthy relationships 99, 101
    help with bottle-feeding 84, 85
pelvic floor exercises 17, 72
pelvic joint pain 35
pet animals 121
physical development
    in the uterus 24–26
    size and weight differences 26, 94
Pilates 18
placenta 13, 25, 29, 30, 36, 62–63

delivery 56, 57, 63, 69, 71
low-lying 64, 65
shared 13, 29, 37
placenta previa 28, 57, 64, 70, 73
play 97, 98
playpens 113
postpartum hemorrhage 63
preeclampsia 28, 36–37, 70
symptoms 32, 36
pregnancy
average pregnancy length 13
belly growth 20, 22–23
complications 36–37
diet and nutrition 14–15
exercise 16–19
finding out you're having twins 10–11
prenatal appointments and tests 28–31
selective termination 31
sex during 23
symptoms 32–35
telling others 10–11
premature babies 25, 60–61
feeding 61, 80, 88, 89
immunizations 121
physical condition 60–61
Special Care 48, 88–89
starting solids 117
premature labor
causes 60, 65
predicting 61
preventing 61
prenatal appointments and tests 28–31
prenatal timetable 29
preparation for twins
baby equipment 42–45
birth plan 40, 48, 58–59
emotional preparation 48–49
hospital bags 40–41
presentation 64–65, 68
progesterone 33, 34
prostaglandin 68

R
rashes and spots 77
reading to your twins 96
relaxation 66
relaxin 16, 34, 35
respiratory distress syndrome (RDS) 61
retinopathy of prematurity 61

S
safety in the home 43, 94, 112–113
second trimester 20, 23, 32
selective termination 31
sex
during pregnancy 23
gender of your babies, finding out 24, 31,

shoes
baby 102
maternity wear 21
shortness of breath 23, 36, 37
siblings 20, 101
behavior difficulties 101
involving 11, 48, 101
side effects of pregnancy 32–35
single parents 101
size and weight differences 26, 94
sleep 106–109
bedtime routine 106–107
co-sleeping 106
crib-sharing 43, 106, 107
during pregnancy 35
naps 109
patterns 108
self-soothing 109
sleeping position 43, 94, 106
sofa snoozing 109
swaddling 108
synchronicity 109
sleeping bags 43
sleep suits 41, 102
smoking 15, 60
social development 97
sofa snoozing 109
Special Care 48, 88–89
spinal blocks 67
sponge bathing 45, 104
starting solids 116–119
statistical chance of having twins 12, 13
stillbirth 15, 36
stork bites 77
stretching exercises 17, 18, 34, 35, 51
strollers 42, 115
Sudden Infant Death Syndrome (SIDS) 15, 77, 109
support networks 86–87
family and friends 46, 47, 48, 86, 101
professional 87
support stockings 34
suppositories 68
swaddling 108
swimming 16, 17
swollen hands and feet 36, 51
symphysis pubic dysfunction 35

T
third trimester 19, 20, 26
3-D scans 24
transcutaneous electrical nerve stimulation (TENS) 66, 67
transverse presentation 64, 65
travel 115
travel cribs 113
travel systems 42
twin-to-twin transfusion syndrome (TTTS) 37

U
ultrasound scans 24, 26, 28, 29, 30
umbilical cord 29, 77
cord prolapse 55, 70, 73
cutting 62
urine tests 31, 37

V
vacuum delivery 62, 67, 69
vaginal delivery 57, 62–63, 64, 65, 68–69
vaginal birth after cesarean (VBAC) 73
vaginal birth plan 58, 59
vaginal discharge 33
variable lie 65
varicose veins 17, 34
vasa previa 70
vegan diet 15
vegetarian diet 14
vernix 77
vitamin and mineral supplements 119
vitamin D 15, 83, 119
vomiting 32, 36

W
walking 17, 19, 34
water breaking 55
amniotomy 68
weight
birth weight 13
pregnancy weight gain 14, 22
regaining pre-pregnancy shape 19, 81
regular weight checkups 120
work 50–51
energy levels 50–51
health risks 50
maternity and parental leave and benefits 51
safety issues 50
time off for childbirth classes 47

Y
yoga 18, 47

Z
zygosity testing 13

Acknowledgments

Katy's Acknowledgments

Peggy Vance, thank you for spotting publishing potential during a fortuitous chance encounter, and for recognizing the need for this book.

I am not sure how many double strollers make it to the Strand or into the inner sanctum of DK, but thank you to everyone who welcomed "me three" whenever we bundled out of our black cab to attend meetings.

Carol, thank you for being my co-author and coffee companion, and for always being only an email away.

Thank you to Noah and Bailey, my twin boys. I am so very proud to be your mommy and love you both more than you could possibly know. And always will.

Finally, thank you to all the members of Team Twin who have held my hand, fed me cake, and kept me sane. THANK YOU!

Carol's Acknowledgments

I would like to add my thanks to editor Laura Palosuo as well as to Helen Murray and Corinne Masciocchi, the previous editors of this book, and above all to my co-author Katy.

Publisher's Acknowledgments

DK would like to thank Angela Baynham for proofreading this book; Marie Lorimer for creating the index; Jo Godfrey-Wood and Carly Churchill for assistance at the photo shoots, Vicky Barnes for hair and makeup; and our models: Soraya and Tamer El Maghraby with Omar and Adam El Maghraby; Tracy and Mike Harvey with Niall and Conor Harvey; Emma-Jane Bartram and Ben Harris with Poppy and Archie Harris; Matthew and Jack Ward; Nikki King with Amy and Millie Ansell; Chinazza and Chizara Jonathan; James and Sam Thompson; Olivia, Emilio and Lottie Brazier; Amity Farrar with Annabel and Brooks Farrar; Sally and Chris Beard with William and Daisy Beard; Helen Murray with Lana and Daniel Casey; Kelly Sharman; Roxanne Schuller; and Liz Cass

Picture Credits

The publisher would like to thank the following for their kind permission to reproduce their photographs:

(Key: a-above; b-below/bottom; c-center; f-far; l-left; r-right; t-top)

10 Corbis: Wavebreak Media Ltd.. 16 Getty Images: Tracy Frankel. 24 Corbis: Mediscan (bl). Science Photo Library: (br). 26 Science Photo Library: Dr Najeeb Layyous. 28 Alamy Images: Ian Hooton / Science Photo Library (bl). Science Photo Library: Ian Hooton (br). 30 Getty Images: Ian Hooton / SPL. 34 Getty Images: Sabine Fritsch (bl). 35 Mother & Baby Picture Library: Ian Hooton. 37 Getty Images: Adam Gault / SPL. 46 Alamy Images: STOCK4B GmbH (bl). Getty Images: Andersen Ross (br). 47 Science Photo Library: B. Boissonnet. 49 Science Photo Library: Ian Hooton. 50 Getty Images: Jamie Grill. 51 Mother & Baby Picture Library: Ian Hooton. 52-53 Getty Images: Tim Hale. 58 Science Photo Library: Tracy Dominey. 60 Alamy Images: Jennie Hart. 62 Corbis: Alexandra Beier / X01172 / Reuters. 68 Alamy Images: Radius Images (br). Mother & Baby Picture Library: Ruth Jenkinson (bl). 69 Science Photo Library: Astier. 70 Alamy Images: Janine Wiedel Photolibrary. 71 Science Photo Library: BSIP, Astier. 72 Alamy Images: Ariel Skelley / Blend Images. 73 Katy Hymas. 88 Alamy Images: Bubbles Photolibrary. 89 Alamy Images: Angela Hampton / Bubbles Photolibrary. 90 Corbis: Jutta Klee. 91 Science Photo Library: AJ Photo. 99 Corbis: Marnie Burkhart. 121 Mother & Baby Picture Library: Ian Hooton

Jacket images: Front: Bella Falk; Back: Corbis: TongRo Image Stock ftl; Photolibrary: Boccabella Debbie tl; Spine: Bella Falk

All other images © Dorling Kindersley
For further information see: www.dkimages.com